The Corn In Green

THE CORN
IS GREEN

A COMEDY IN THREE ACTS BY

EMLYN WILLIAMS

RANDOM HOUSE · NEW YORK

'First Printing

Illustrations courtesy of VANDAMM STUDIO

COPYRIGHT, 1938, 1941, BY EMLYN WILLIAMS

To

S. G. C.

AND, AT HER REQUEST,

TO ALL TEACHERS.

The Corn Is Green was first produced at the National Theatre, New York City, on November 26, 1940, with the following cast:

(In the order in which they speak)

John Goronwy Jones	RHYS WILLIAMS
Miss Ronberry	MILDRED DUNNOCK
Idwal Morris	CHARLES S. PURSELL
Sarah Pugh	GWYNETH HUGHES
A Groom	GEORGE BLEASDALE
The Squire	EDMOND BREON
Mrs. Watty	ROSALIND IVAN
Bessie Watty	THELMA SCHNEE
Miss Moffat	ETHEL BARRYMORE
Robbart Robbatch	THOMAS LYONS
Morgan Evans	RICHARD WARING
Glyn Thomas	KENNETH CLARKE
John Owen	MERRITT O'DUEL
Will Hughes	TERENCE MORGAN
Old Tom	SAYRE CRAWLEY

Boys, Girls and Parents: Julia Knox, Amelia Romano, Betty Conibear, Rosalind Carter, Harda Normann, Joseph McInerney, Marcel Dill, Gwilym Williams, Tommy Dix.

Produced and staged by HERMAN SHUMLIN
Setting designed by HOWARD BAY
Costumes designed by ERNEST SCHRAPPS

SCENES

ACT ONE

Scene I—An afternoon in June.
Scene II—A night in August, six weeks later.

ACT TWO

Scene I—An early evening in August, two years later.
Scene II—A morning in November, three months later.

ACT THREE

An afternoon in July, seven months later.

———

The action of the play takes place in the living room of a house in Glansarno, a small village in a remote Welsh countryside.

The time is the latter part of the last century, and covers a period of three years.

ACT ONE

ACT ONE

Scene I

The living room of a house in Glansarno, a small village in a remote Welsh countryside. A sunny afternoon in June, in the latter part of the last century.

The house is old, and the ceiling slants away from the audience. Facing the audience, on the left, narrow stairs lead up to a landing and then on the left to a passage to the bedrooms; we can just see, facing, the door of one bedroom which is later to be Miss Moffat's. A door leads to the kitchen; at the foot of the stairs, an alcove and a door lead to a little room which is later the study. In the back wall, to the right, the front door, with outside it a small stone porch faintly overgrown with ivy, and opening to the left on to a path; in the back wall, to the left, a large bay window with a small sofa seat. In the right wall, downstage, the garden door, and above it a small side window; when the door is open we can just see a trellised porch with a creeper. Through the thickish curtains over the bay window we glimpse a jagged stone wall and the sky.

The floor is of stone flags, with one rug in front of the sofa. Faded sprigged wallpaper.

The furniture is a curious jumble of old Welsh and Victorian pieces. A large serviceable flat-topped desk under the side window, a desk-chair in front of it; a table with a small chair, near the middle of the room; an armchair, between the desk and the table; a sofa, downstage, between the table and

3

the foot of the stairs; in the back wall, near the kitchen door, an old Welsh dresser with plates and crockery; in the left wall, against the staircase, a settle; in the window recess, a small table. In the back wall, to the right of the front door, a small grandfather's clock. An oil lamp on the center table, another on the desk. Another on the dresser.

The most distinctive feature of the room is the amount of books on the walls, of all sorts and sizes; some in open bookcases, others on newly built shelves, in practically every available space.

The kitchen door is open; there are books on the window seat.

As the curtain rises, MR. JOHN GORONWY JONES *and* MISS RONBERRY *are arranging the last books in their places; she is sitting on a tiny stool taking books out of a large packing case and fitting them on to narrow shelves between the garden door and the side window, flicking each one mechanically with a tiny lace handkerchief. She is a gentlewoman in her thirties, with the sort of pinched prettiness that tends to look sharp before that age, especially when it makes sporadic attempts at coquetry; she wears a hat. He is a shabby Welshman of forty, bespectacled, gloomy and intense; a volcano, harmless even in full eruption. He is perched on top of a stepladder, arranging books on a high shelf between the front door and the bay window, dusting them vigorously before putting them in place.*

MR. JONES
(*Singing*)
". . . Pechudur wyf, y dua'n fyw—'O Uffern!' yw fy nghri; Gostwng dy glust, a'am llefain clyw . . . So—so—so—la—so—sol!"

4

MISS RONBERRY

(*Seated on stool*)

Your voice has given me an agonizing headache. And if you must indulge in music, will you please not do it in Welsh?

MR. JONES

I wasn't indulgin' in music, I was singin' a hymn. (*Putting the last book on the shelf and climbing down*) And if a hymn gives you a headache, there is nothing wrong with the hymn, there is something wrong with your head.

MISS RONBERRY

I still don't see the necessity for it.

MR. JONES

(*Picking up the empty packing case and moving toward the kitchen*)

I sing to cheer myself up.

MISS RONBERRY

What do the words mean?

MR. JONES

"The wicked shall burn in hell." (*Exits into kitchen.*)

(MISS RONBERRY *picks up packing case.* IDWAL MORRIS *comes in from garden, stops at door.*)

MISS RONBERRY

Oh! (IDWAL *is a thin, ragged boy of thirteen, very timid*) Is the garden nice and ready?

THE CORN IS GREEN

IDWAL

'Sgwelwchi'n dda, d'wi'di torri'r bloda.

MISS RONBERRY

Translation! (*Crosses with box to chair in arch of bay window—then to left of center table.*)

(MR. JONES *returns, carries two piles of books.*)

IDWAL

Os gwelwchi'n dda, Mistar Jones, d'wi'di torri'r bloda, a mae'r domen yn hogla'n ofnadwy.

(MISS RONBERRY *goes to him and takes flowers.*)

MR. JONES

He says he cut the sweet peas and the rubbish heap is smelling terrible.

MISS RONBERRY

Oh, dear. His father must put something on it. (*Arranges flowers in vase.*)

MR. JONES
(*Going up ladder*)

That's the English all over. The devil is there, is he? Don't take him away, put a bit of scent on him! Gofyn i dy dad i roi rwbeth arno am heddyw.

IDWAL

Diolch, syr. (*He runs into the garden again.*)

MISS RONBERRY

I hope he will have the sense to give the message.

MR. JONES

(*Still on ladder*)

It is terrible, isn't it, the people on these green fields and flowery hillsides bein' turned out of Heaven because they cannot answer Saint Peter when he asks them who they are in English? It is wicked, isn't it, the Welsh children not bein' *born* knowing English—isn't it? Good heavens, God bless my soul, by Jove, this, that and the other!

MISS RONBERRY

Anybody in Wales will tell you that the people in this part of the countryside are practically barbarians. (SARAH PUGH *comes out of the bedroom and down the stairs. She is a buxom peasant woman, with a strong Welsh accent*) Not a single caller for fifteen miles, and even then . . .

SARAH

Please, Miss—I made the bed lovely. And I dust . . .

MISS RONBERRY

That will be all, dear. The Colonel is bound to have his own manservant.

SARAH

Then I better have another sit down in my post office.

MR. JONES

What is the matter with your post office?

7

SARAH

It has—(*Opens door*)—not had a letter for seven weeks. Nobody but me can write, and no good *me* writin', because nobody but me can read. If I get a telegram I put him in the window and I die straight off. (*She goes, closes door.*)

MISS RONBERRY

You see? I can't *think* why a Colonel should elect to come and live in this place. There. . . . I have never *seen* so many books! I do hope the curtains will not be too feminine. I chose them with such care.

MR. JONES
(*Darkly*)

Why are you taking so much trouble getting somebody else's house ready for them?

MISS RONBERRY
(*Examines cushion*)

You need not have helped me if you did not wish! (*Crosses to settle for needle and thread*) I am frightened of the spinning-wheel, too, and the china; his own furniture is *so* distinctive. The desk. And the wastepaper basket. . . . So . . so virile.

MR. JONES
(*On ladder*)

Are you hoping that the Colonel will live up to his waste paper basket?

MISS RONBERRY

That is horrid.

8

MR. JONES

And then you will have two on a string: him and the Squire . . .

MISS RONBERRY

Mr. Jones!

MR. JONES

And if I was a bit more of a masher, there would be three. Worldly things, that is your trouble. "Please, Mistar Jones, my life is as empty as a rotten nutshell, so get me a husband before it is too late, double quick!"

(*A knock at the front door; it opens and a liveried* GROOM *appears.*)

MISS RONBERRY

You insulting man . . .

GROOM

The Squire.

(*The* SQUIRE *follows him. He is a handsome English country gentleman in his forties, wearing knickerbockers and gaiters; a hard drinker, bluff, kind, immensely vain; and, when the time comes, obtusely obstinate. The* GROOM *goes out again and shuts the door.*)

MISS RONBERRY

(*Fluttering eagerly into a handshake*)

Squire. . . .

9

THE CORN IS GREEN

THE SQUIRE

(With exuberant patronage)

Delicious lady, delicious surprise, and a merry afternoon to
ye, as our forebears put it. . . . How are you, Jones, making
the most of your half-day?

MR. JONES

*(Sullenly, making an uncertain effort to rise from the
ladder)*

Good afternoon, sir . . .

THE SQUIRE

Squat, dear fellow, squat . . . No ceremony with me!
And why, dear lady, were you not at the Travers-Ellis wedding?

(JONES starts down the ladder.)

MISS RONBERRY

Naughty! I sat next to you at the breakfast.

THE SQUIRE

By Jingo! So you did!

MR. JONES

Excuse me . . .

(He goes into study.)

THE SQUIRE

Deuced fine breakfast. . . .

MISS RONBERRY

We had a talk about children.

THE SQUIRE

Did we? Well, the next wedding we're at, there'll be *no* chance of my forgettin' you, eh?

MISS RONBERRY

Why?

THE SQUIRE

Because—you'll be the stunning, blushing bride!

MISS RONBERRY

And who—will be the—?

THE SQUIRE

Now that's what *I* want to know, because *I'm* going to give you away!

MISS RONBERRY

Oh!

(MR. JONES *returns from the study.*)

THE SQUIRE

Now who's it going to be?

MISS RONBERRY

Squire, you are too impatient! I am taking my time!

THE SQUIRE

Too bad . . . No sign of the new inhabitant?

MISS RONBERRY

Any moment now, I think! The pony and trap met the London train at a quarter to twelve!

THE SQUIRE

Hasn't the fellow got his own private conveyance?

MISS RONBERRY

I think not.

THE SQUIRE

I hope he's all right.

MISS RONBERRY

He wrote very civilly to Mr. Jones about the house . . .

THE SQUIRE

Oh, yes. Not a club, I remember, but the paper—not bad texture. Funny sort of chap, though, eh?

MISS RONBERRY

Why?

THE SQUIRE

All these books.

(*A timid knock at the front door.* IDWAL *enters, very frightened.*)

IDWAL

Os gwelwchi'n dda, syr, mae Mistar Tomos wedi 'ngyrru i yma ich gweld chi!

THE SQUIRE

Y'know, it's as bad as being abroad. . . . Been among it
half my life, and never get used to it.

MR. JONES

The groom told him, sir, that you wanted to see him.

THE SQUIRE

Oh, yes—well, come here where I can see you, eh? (SQUIRE
turns to him) Now, boy, how old are you— (*To* JONES)—or
whatever the Chinese is for it?

MR. JONES

Just turned thirteen, sir.

THE SQUIRE

Thirteen? Well, why aren't you working in the mine over
in the next valley? Don't like to see young fellows wasting
their time, y'know.

MR. JONES

He has got one lung funny.

THE SQUIRE

Oh, I see. . . . Rough luck. Here, laddy, there's a sixpence
for you, and remember all work and no play makes Taffy
a dull boy!

IDWAL

Diolch yn faw, syr . . .

THE SQUIRE

And tell your uncle I want Ranger shod . . .

IDWAL

Diolch, syr . . .

THE SQUIRE

And a gate mended . . .

IDWAL

Diolch yn faw, syr . . . (*He runs out.*)

MISS RONBERRY

But he hasn't understood your orders!

THE SQUIRE

Neither he has . . .

MR. JONES

He thought the Squire was havin' a chat. I will tell his
uncle—

IDWAL

(*Offstage, calling shrilly to his friends*)

Tomos—Aneurin—dyma'r cerbyd— (JONES *looks out window*)—dewch i wel'd—fe ddwe-dai wrth y Scweiar—hry-
siwch!

MISS RONBERRY

(*Rises*)

That must be something . . .

(IDWAL *appears at the front door, panting with expec-
tation.*)

IDWAL

Pliss, syr, dyma'r carbyd!

(*He darts back, leaving the door open.*)

14

MISS RONBERRY
(Looks out window)
He must mean the Colonel. How gratifying . . .

(BESSIE WATTY *wanders shyly in. She is an extremely pretty, plump little girl of fourteen; it is a moment before one realizes that her demureness is too good to be true. She wears her hair over her shoulders, is dressed very plainly, in a shabby sailor suit and hat, and carries brown-paper parcels. She is followed* by MRS. WATTY, *a middle-aged Cockney servant, dressed for traveling, carrying a hamper in her arms. Her self-confidence is not so overwhelming as the* Squire's, *but it is quite as complete, and as kindly.)*

THE SQUIRE
Capital . . .

MRS. WATTY
(To the SQUIRE)
D'you speak English?

THE SQUIRE
(Taken aback)
I do.

MRS. WATTY
Be a dear an' 'old this!
(She hands him the hamper and hurries out through the front door.)

THE SQUIRE
Crikey! A Colonel with an abigail! (*Catching* BESSIE'S *owl-*

15

like expression and stopping short) Why don't *you* say something?

BESSIE

I never speak till I'm spoken to.

THE SQUIRE

Oh . . . Well, who was that?

BESSIE

My mummy. (*To* MISS RONBERRY) I never had no daddy. (*Her accent is not as natural as her mother's; she sometimes strains to be ladylike, especially at moments like this.* MRS. WATTY *returns with two large parcels.*)

MRS. WATTY

My Gawd—(*Pause*)—they're heavy. (*Puts them on table.*)

MISS RONBERRY

What are they?

MRS. WATTY

Books.

(*Takes hamper from* SQUIRE.)

THE SQUIRE

Is your employer with you, my good woman?

MRS. WATTY

No, followed be'ind, most of the way. Ought to be 'ere by now, I'll 'ave a see. . . . (*Goes to door*) 'Ere we are! Tally-o! Thought we'd lost you!

(*A pause.* MISS MOFFAT *comes in from the road, wheel-ing a bicycle. She is about forty, a healthy English-woman with an honest face, clear, beautiful eyes, a humorous mouth, a direct friendly manner, and un-bounded vitality, which is prevented from tiring the spectator by its capacity for sudden silences and for listening. Her most prominent characteristic is her complete unsentimentality. She wears a straw hat, collar and tie, and a dark unexaggerated skirt; a satchel hangs from her shoulder.*)

MISS MOFFAT

I was hoping to pass you, but that last hill was too much for me. (*Displaying the bicycle*) Good afternoon.

ALL

Good afternoon.

MISS MOFFAT

There's a smallish crowd already, so I thought I'd better bring Priscilla inside. Watty, can you find somewhere for her? (*She gives the room a quick appraising look, peers out of the side window, and nods pleasantly to the* SQUIRE.)

MRS. WATTY

Dunno, I'm sure.

MISS MOFFAT

I think I'll have a look at the garden first. (*She goes out out into the garden.*)

MRS. WATTY

(*Wheeling bicycle gingerly toward the kitchen*)
That must be my kitchen in there, we'll 'ave to 'ang 'er

with the bacon. (*To* BESSIE) Come on, girl, give us a 'and—don't stand there gettin' into mischief!

BESSIE

I'm frightened of it.

MRS. WATTY

It won't bite you! Most it can do is catch fire, and I'll 'ave a drop o' water ready for it. (*Her voice fades away into the kitchen.*)

BESSIE

Has anybody got a sweetie?

MISS RONBERRY

No.

BESSIE

Oh. . . .

(*She trails after her mother into the kitchen.* MISS MOFFAT *returns very businesslike.*)

MISS MOFFAT

It's bigger than I expected. . . . (*Closes door*) There! (*Puts satchel on desk*) Good afternoon! So this is my house. . . .

THE SQUIRE
(*Blustering*)

No, it isn't!

MISS MOFFAT

Oh? Isn't this Pengarth? The name of the building, I mean?

MISS RONBERRY

Yes, it is. . . .

MISS MOFFAT

That's right, it was left me by my uncle, Dr. Moffat. I'm Miss Moffat. I take it you're Miss Ronberry, who so kindly corresponded with me?

THE SQUIRE

But sure—those letters were written by a man?

MISS MOFFAT

Well, if they were, I have been grossly deceiving myself for over forty years. Now this is jolly interesting. Why did it never occur to you that I might be a woman?

THE SQUIRE

Well—the paper wasn't scented . . .

MISS RONBERRY

And such a bold hand . . .

THE SQUIRE

And that long piece about the lease being ninety-nine years, don't you know . . .

MISS MOFFAT

Was there anything wrong with it?

THE SQUIRE

No, there wasn't, that's the point.

19

THE CORN IS GREEN

MISS MOFFAT

I see.

MISS RONBERRY

And surely you signed your name very oddly?

MISS MOFFAT

My initials, L. C. Moffat? You see, I've never felt that Lily Christabel really suited me.

MISS RONBERRY

And I thought—it meant Lieutenant-Colonel! But there *was* a military title after it.

MISS MOFFAT

M.A., Master of Arts.

THE SQUIRE

Arts? D'ye mean the degree my father bought me when I came down from the Varsity?

MISS MOFFAT

The very same. Except that I was at Aberdeen, and had to work jolly hard for mine.

THE SQUIRE

A female M.A.? And how long's that going to last?

MISS MOFFAT

Quite a long time, I hope, considering we've been waiting for it for two thousand years.

MR. JONES

(*Who has been silent since she entered*)

Are you saved?

MISS MOFFAT

(*Starting, turning and taking him in for the first time*)

I beg your pardon?

MR. JONES

Are you Church or Chapel?

MISS MOFFAT

I really don't know . . . And now you know all about me, what do *you* do?

THE SQUIRE

I'm afraid I don't do anything. (*He extricates his hat angrily from the table.*)

MISS RONBERRY

Mr. Treverby owns the Hall!

MISS MOFFAT

Really. I've never had much to do with the landed gentry. Interesting.

THE SQUIRE

Au revoir, dear lady. 'Day, Jones. (*He goes frigidly out by the front door.* JONES *closes door.*)

MISS MOFFAT

Well, nobody could say that I've made a conquest there. . . . What's the matter with him?

(MRS. WATTY *comes in from kitchen with tea tray.*)

MRS. WATTY

I found the tea, ma'am, it *looks* all right. . . .

MISS MOFFAT

Good!

MRS. WATTY

An' the big luggage is comin' after . . .

MISS MOFFAT
(*At study door*)

This isn't a bad little room . . .

MRS. WATTY

Where's his lordship?

MISS MOFFAT
(*Going upstairs*)

Took offense and left. (*She disappears down the passage.*)

MRS. WATTY
(*Looks at them both*)

Took offense? At 'er?

MISS RONBERRY

I am afraid so.

MRS. WATTY

I'm jiggered! What d'*you* think of 'er, eh? Ain't she a clinker?

MISS RONBERRY

She is unusual, is she not?

MRS. WATTY

She's a clinker, that's what Terrible strong-willed, o' course, terrible. Get 'er into mischief, I keep tellin' 'er. Would bring me 'ere. I said no, I said, not with my past, I said.

MISS RONBERRY

Your past?

MRS. WATTY

Before she took me up. But what with 'er, and now I've joined the Corpse, it's all blotted out.

MR. JONES

The Corpse?

MRS. WATTY

The Militant Righteous Corpse. Ran into 'em in the street I did, singin' and prayin' and collectin', full blast; and I been a different woman since. Are *you* saved?

MR. JONES

Yes, I am.

MRS. WATTY

So'm I. Ain't it lovely?

MISS RONBERRY

But what *was*—your past?

MRS. WATTY
(*Sorrowfully*)

Light fingers.

MISS RONBERRY

Light fingers? You mean—stealing?

MRS. WATTY

Everywhere I went. Terrible. Pennies, stockin's, brooches, spoons, tiddly, anything. Every time there was a do, everything went; and I always knew it was me! (MISS MOFFAT *comes downstairs*) I was just tellin' 'em about my trouble.

MISS MOFFAT

Well, don't tell them any more. Is your kitchen all right?

MRS. WATTY

I ain't seed no mice yet. (*She goes into kitchen, takes hamper with her.*)

(*Far away, softly, the sound of boys' voices, singing an old country song, in harmony, in Welsh: "Yr Hufen Melyn."*)

MISS MOFFAT

I agree with the last tenant's taste. . . . You have arranged my things quite splendidly, Miss Ronberry. I do thank you—both of you. . . . I like this house (*As the music grows imperceptibly in the distance*) . . . What's that singing?

MR JONES

Boys coming home from the mine.

MISS RONBERRY

They burst into song on the slightest provocation. You mustn't take any notice . . .

MISS MOFFAT

I like it . . . And those mountains. That grand wild coun-

tryside . . . The foreign-looking people . . . But business . . .
I've heard about that mine. How far is it?

MR. JONES

It is the Glasynglo coal mine, six miles over the hills.

MISS MOFFAT

Hm . . .

MISS RONBERRY

We're hoping it will stay the only one, or our scenery will
be ruined—such a pretty landscape . . .

MISS MOFFAT

What is the large empty building next door?

MR. JONES

Next door? The old barn belongin' to the Gwalia Farm,
before the farm was burnt down. . . .

(*Song fades out.*)

MISS MOFFAT

So it's free?

MR. JONES
(*Perplexed*)

Free? Yes . . .

MISS RONBERRY
(*Rises*)

I am overstaying my welcome. So very charming . . .

MR. JONES

I also. All the volumes are dusted. . . .
(*Starts to go toward her.*)

MISS MOFFAT

I want you two people. Very specially. First you, Miss Ronberry. I used to meet friends of yours at lectures in London. You live alone, you have just enough money, you're not badly educated, and time lies heavy on your hands.

MISS RONBERRY

The Wingroves! How mean! I should never have thought . . .

MISS MOFFAT

Isn't that so?

MISS RONBERRY

Not at all. When the right gentleman appears . . .

MISS MOFFAT

If you're a spinster well on in her thirties, he's lost his way and isn't coming. Why don't you face the fact and enjoy yourself, the same as I do?

MISS RONBERRY

But when did you give up hope? Oh, what a horrid expression. . . .

MISS MOFFAT

I can't recall ever having any hope. Visitors used to take a long look at my figure and say: "*She's* going to be the clever one."

MISS RONBERRY

But a woman's only future is to marry and—and fulfill the duties of . . .

MISS MOFFAT

Skittles! I'd have made a shocking wife, anyway.

MISS RONBERRY

But haven't you ever—been in love?

MISS MOFFAT

No.

MISS RONBERRY

How very odd.

MISS MOFFAT

I've never talked to a man for more than five minutes without wanting to box his ears.

MISS RONBERRY

But how have you passed your time since . . . ?

MISS MOFFAT

Since I had no hope? Very busily. In the East End, for years.

MISS RONBERRY

Social service?

MISS MOFFAT

If you like; though there's nothing very social about washing invalids with every unmentionable ailment under the sun. . . . I've read a lot, too. I'm afraid I'm what is known as an educated woman. Which brings me to Mr. Jones; the Wingroves told me all about you, too.

THE CORN IS GREEN

MR. JONES

My conscience is as clear as the snow.

MISS MOFFAT

I'm sure it is, but you're a disappointed man, aren't you?

MR. JONES
(*Startled*)

How can I be disappointed when I am saved?

MISS MOFFAT

Oh, but you can! You can't really enjoy sitting all by your-self on a raft, on a sea, containing everybody you know. You're disappointed because you're between two stools.

MR. JONES

Between two stools? On a raft?

MISS MOFFAT

Exactly. Your father was a grocer with just enough money to send you to a grammar school, with the result that you are educated beyond your sphere, and yet fail to qualify for the upper classes. You feel frustrated, and fall back on being saved. Am I right?

MR. JONES

It is such a terrible thing you have said that I will have to think it over.

MISS MOFFAT

Do. (*Rises*) But in the meantime—(*Pause*)—would you two like to stop moping and be very useful to me?

28

MISS RONBERRY

Useful?

MISS MOFFAT

Yes, tell me—within a radius of five miles, how many families are there round here?

MISS RONBERRY

Families? There's the Squire, of course, and Mrs. Gwent-Price in the little Plas Lodge, quite a dear thing . . .

MISS MOFFAT

I mean ordinary people.

MISS RONBERRY

The villagers?

MISS MOFFAT

Yes. How many families?

MISS RONBERRY

I really haven't the faint . . .

MR. JONES

There are about twenty families in the village and fifteen in the farms around.

MISS MOFFAT

Many children?

MR. JONES

What age?

MISS MOFFAT

Up to sixteen or seventeen.

MR. JONES

Round here they are only children till they are twelve.
Then they are sent away over the hills to the mine, and in
one week they are old men.

MISS MOFFAT

I see. How many can read or write?

MR. JONES

Next to none.

MISS RONBERRY

Why do you ask?

MISS MOFFAT

Because I am going to start a school for them.

MISS RONBERRY
(*Coldly*)
Start a school for them? What for?

MISS MOFFAT

What for? See these books? Hundreds of 'em, and something wonderful to read in every single one. These nippers
are to be cut off from all that, for ever, are they? Why? Because they happen to be born penniless in an uncivilized
countryside, coining gold down there in that stinking dun-
geon for some beef-headed old miser!

30

MR. JONES
(*Roused*)

That's right. . . .

MISS MOFFAT

The printed page, what is it? One of the miracles of all time, that's what! And yet when these poor babbies set eyes on it, they might just as well have been struck by the miracle of sudden blindness; and that, to my mind, is plain infamous!

MR. JONES

My goodness, Miss, that's right. . . .

MISS RONBERRY

The *ordinary* children, you mean?

MISS MOFFAT

Yes, my dear, the ordinary children that came into the world by the same process exactly as you and I. When I heard that this part of the world was a disgrace to a Christian country, I knew this house was a godsend. I am going to start a school, immediately, next door in the barn, and you are going to help me!

MISS RONBERRY

I?

MISS MOFFAT

Yes, you! You're going to fling away your parasol and your kid gloves, and you're going to stain those tapering fingers with a little honest toil!

MISS RONBERRY

I couldn't teach those children, I couldn't! They—they smell!

MISS MOFFAT

If we'd never been taught to wash, so would we; we'll put 'em under the pump. . . . Mr. Jones—d'ye know what I'm going to do with that obstinate old head of yours?

MR. JONES

My head?

MISS MOFFAT

I'm going to crack it open with a skewer. And I'm going to excavate all those chunks of grammar-school knowledge, give 'em a quick dust, and put 'em to some use at last.

MR. JONES

I am a solicitor's clerk in Gwaenygam and I earn thirty-three shillings per week. . . .

MISS MOFFAT

I'll give you thirty-four—and your lunch.

MISS RONBERRY

I have an enormous house to run, and the flowers to do. . . .

MISS MOFFAT

Shut it up except one room, and leave the flowers to die a natural death—in their own beds. I've been left a little money and I know exactly what I am going to do with it. . . .

MR. JONES

But those children are in the mine—earning money. How can they . . . ?

MISS MOFFAT

I'll pay their parents the few miserable pennies they get out of it . . . And when I've finished with you, *you* won't have time to think about snapping up a husband, and *you* won't have time to be so pleased that you're saved! Well?

MR. JONES

I do not care if you are not chapel, I am with you.

MISS MOFFAT

Good! I have all the details worked out. I'll explain roughly. . . . Come along—my dears, gather round, children—gather round. (*She takes the dazed* MISS RONBERRY *by the arm, seats her beside her on the sofa, and beckons* MR. JONES *to sit on her other side*) Of course, we must go slowly at first, but if we put our backs into it . . . Here we are, three stolid middle-aged folk, settled in our little groove and crammed with benefits; and *there* are those babbies scarcely out of the shell, that have no idea they are even breathing the air. . . . Only God can know how their life will end, but He will give us the chance to direct them a little of the way. . . .

MR. JONES

(*Intoning, seized with religious fervor*)

We have the blessed opportunity to raise up the children from the bowels of the earth where the devil hath imprisoned

33

them in the powers of darkness, and bring them to the light of knowledge—

MRS. WATTY

(*Coming in from the kitchen*)

Here's the tea!

MISS MOFFAT

Each of us can take several classes, not only for the children, but their fathers and their mothers, and the older people too.

The curtain falls.

ACT ONE

Scene II

A night in August, six weeks later. The window curtains are closed and the lamps lit. The armchair has been pushed away from table, and two small benches face the audience. Red geraniums in pots across the window sills. Miss Moffat's straw hat is slung over the knob of the settle at the foot of the stairs. The big desk, the sofa and the settle are littered with books, exercise books and sheets of paper. Apart from these details the room is unchanged.

Sitting on the bench are five black-faced miners, between twelve and sixteen years of age, wearing caps, mufflers, boots and corduroys embedded in coal; they look as if they had been commanded to wait. They all look alike under their black; the ringleader is MORGAN EVANS, *fifteen, quick and impudent; his second is* ROBBART ROBBATCH, *a big, slow boy, a year or two older; the others are* GLYN THOMAS, WILL HUGHES *and* JOHN OWEN. *They all hum at rise.*

MRS. WATTY *comes downstairs, carrying a basket of washing.*

MRS. WATTY

You 'ere again? (*On stairs, stops halfway down.*)

ROBBART

Be mai'n ddeud?

MRS. WATTY

I said, you 'ere again?

35

MORGAN

No, Miss.

MRS. WATTY

What d'ye mean, no, Miss?

MORGAN

We issn't 'ere again, Miss.

MRS. WATTY

What are you, then?

MORGAN

We issn't the same lot ass this mornin', Miss.

MRS. WATTY

Ain't you?

MORGAN

Miss Ronny-berry tell us to wait, Miss.

MRS. WATTY

Ma'am! (*Goes to kitchen door.*)

MISS MOFFAT
(*In the bedroom*)

Yes?

MRS. WATTY

Five more nigger boys for you! (*She goes into the kitchen. MORGAN takes a bottle from his pocket and swigs at it. One of the others holds out his hand, takes the bottle, gulps, and gives it back, while another begins to hum, absent-mindedly,*

36

a snatch of the same song as before. The rest take up the harmony and sing it to the end. MR. JONES *comes in.*)

MORGAN

Sh! Good evenin', sir.

MR. JONES

Good evening. (*Tips hat.*)

MORGAN

I seed you and the lady teacher be'ind the door! (*A laugh from him and the others.*)

MR. JONES

You wait till you see Miss Moffat. She will give you what for.

MORGAN

(*Shaking finger at boys*)

You wait till you see Miss Moffat. She will give you what for! (MR. JONES *goes into the kitchen.* ROBBART *repeats:* "You wait till you see Miss Moffat, she will give you what for!") Shh!

(MISS MOFFAT *comes downstairs from the bedroom.*)

MISS MOFFAT

I told you, the shape of the bedroom doesn't allow for a door into the barn—Oh, she isn't here. . . . Sorry to keep you waiting, boys, but I have to go across to Mr. Rees, the carpenter, and then I'll be able to talk to you. In the meantime, will you go to the pump in the garden shed, and wash your hands? Through there. You'll find a lantern. Did you understand all that?

MORGAN

Yes, Miss.

THE OTHERS

Thank you, Miss.

MISS MOFFAT

Good. (*Starts to go.*)

MORGAN

Please, Miss, can I have a kiss?

MISS MOFFAT
(*Returns*)

What did you say?

MORGAN

Please, Miss, can I have a kiss?

MISS MOFFAT

Of course you can. (*Puts her foot on bench—takes him by the neck and bends him over her knee and spanks him with the plans she carries*) Can I oblige anybody else? (*She goes out by the front door. The others follow her with their eyes, aghast, in silence.*)

ROBBART

Please, Miss, can I 'ave a smack bottom?

(*An uproar of mirth, and a quick tangle of Welsh.*)

WILL

Na-beth of Naw-stee.

MORGAN

Cythral uffarn . . .

GLYN

Be harı hi—hı a'ı molchı . . .

JOHN

Pwy sisho molchı . . .

WILL

Welso ti'rioed wraıg fel ene—

MORGAN

Mae'n lwcus na ddaru mi mo'ı thrawo hi lawr a'ı lladd
hı . . .

ROBBART

Nawn—(*Rises*)—i drio molchi—dewch hogıa— (*All rise—
start off*) mae'n well nag eistedd yma—dewch . . .

GLYN

Dynna gusan ytı Morgan Bach.

ROBBART

Cymmer yna y corgu fol.

JOHN

Dynna ateb—i—ti.

WILL

Jobin da y diawl.

MORGAN

Cai da geg.

39

THE CORN IS GREEN

(*They lumber into the garden, close door.* MR. JONES'
*head appears timidly from the kitchen. He sees they
are gone, gives a sigh of relief, and comes into the
room, carrying books.* BESSIE *comes in from the front
door, dejected and sulky. She is munching a sweet;
her hair is in curls, and one curl is turned around one
finger, which she holds stiffly in the air. She lays her
hat on the sofa, then decides* MR. JONES's *company is
better than none.*)

BESSIE

Would you like a sweetie?

MR. JONES

No, thank you, my little dear. Have you had another walk?

BESSIE

Yes, Mr. Jones. All by myself.

MR. JONES

Did you see anybody?

BESSIE

Only a lady and a gentleman in the lane—and mother told
me never to look. . . . I do miss the shops. London's full o'
them, you know.

MR. JONES

Full of fancy rubbish, you mean.

BESSIE

I'd like to be always shopping, I would. Sundays and
all. . . .

MRS. WATTY

Bessie!

BESSIE

(*Slyly*)

Mr. Jones, is it true the school idea isn't going on that well?

MR. JONES

Who told you that?

BESSIE

Miss Ronberry was sayin' something to my mum. Oh, I wasn't listenin'! . . . Besides, we've been here six weeks, and nothin's started yet.

MR. JONES

Everything is splendid.

BESSIE

(*Disappointed*)

Oh, I'm glad. Miss Moffat's been cruel to me, but I don't bear no grudge.

MR. JONES

Cruel to you?

BESSIE

She hides my sweets. She's a liar too.

MR. JONES

A liar?

BESSIE

Told me they're bad for me. And it says on the bag they're nourishin'. . . . And the idea of learnin' school with those children, ooh . . .

41

MR. JONES

Why are you holding your hair like that?

BESSIE

These are my curls. D'you think it's nice?

MR. JONES

It is nice, but it is wrong.

MRS. WATTY

(*Calling shrilly, in the kitchen*)

Bess-ie!

BESSIE

I've been curlin' each one round me finger and holdin' it tight till it was all right. My finger's achin' something terrible. (*She goes into the kitchen. A knock at the front door.*)

MR. JONES

Dewch ifewn.

(IDWAL *appears, drawing a small wooden crate on tiny wheels which he pushes in front of the sofa.* MISS RONBERRY *comes in from the study.*)

IDWAL

Cloch yr ysgol, Mistar Jones.

MR. JONES

Diolch, ymachgeni. (*Pause*) Nosdawch.

IDWAL

Nosdawch, Mistar Jones. (*He leaves through the front door.*)

MISS RONBERRY

It says here that eight sevens are fifty-six. Then it says that seven eights are fifty-six—I can't see that at all. (MISS MOFFAT *returns.*) Well?

MISS MOFFAT

No good.

MISS RONBERRY

Oh, dear.

MISS MOFFAT

Mr. Rees says he's had a strict order not to discuss lining the roof till the lease of the barn is signed.

MR. JONES

Who gave the order?

MISS MOFFAT

That's what I want to know.

MISS RONBERRY

And when will the lease be signed?

MISS MOFFAT

Never, it seems to me. Did you call at the solicitor's?

MR. JONES

They have located Sir Herbert Vezey, but he is now doubtful about letting the barn and will give his decision by post.

43

MISS MOFFAT

But why? He'd already said it was no use to him. And my references were impeccable. . . . *Why?*

MISS RONBERRY

You look tired.

MISS MOFFAT

It's been a bit of a day. A letter from the mine to say no child can be released aboveground—that's all blethers, but still . . . A request from the public house not to start a school in case it interferes with beer-swilling and games of chance. A message from the chapel people to the effect that I am a foreign adventuress with cloven feet; a bit of a day.

(MRS. WATTY *comes in from the kitchen with a cup of tea.*)

MRS. WATTY

Drop o' tea, ma'am, I expect you've 'ad a bit of a day. . . .

MISS MOFFAT

Who was that at the back, anything important?

MRS. WATTY

Only the person that does for that Mrs. Gwent-Price. Would you not 'ave your school opposite her lady because of her lady's 'eadaches.

MISS MOFFAT
(*Angrily*)

What did you say?

44

MRS. WATTY

I pulverized 'er. I said it would be a shame, I said, if there was such a shindy over the way that the village couldn't hear Mrs. Double-Barrel givin' her 'usband what for, I said. The person didn't know where to put 'erself. (*She goes back into the kitchen.*)

MR. JONES

That has not helped the peace in the community, neither.

MISS MOFFAT

I know, but she does make a tip-top cup of tea. . . . (*Seeing the crate, wearily*) What's that?

MR. JONES

It is the bell, for the school.

MISS MOFFAT

Oh, is it?

MISS RONBERRY
(*Rising*)
The bell? Do let us have a peep . . .

MR. JONES

It was on Llantalon Monastery before it burnt down. . . .

MISS MOFFAT
(*Opens crate*)
Look, it's got the rope, and everything. . . . Well, it's good to see it, anyway.

45

MISS RONBERRY

The mason finished the little tower for it yesterday. Do let us tell those boys to put it up! It'll bring us luck!

MISS MOFFAT

If it keeps them out of mischief till I'm ready . . .

MISS RONBERRY

Mr. Jones, do go and tell them!

(JONES *gives her a doubtful look and goes toward the garden. As he opens the door,* JOHN OWEN *shouts:* "Mai, Mr. Jones, yn dywed." *All the boys laugh.*)

MISS MOFFAT

Poor Jonesy, he's terrified of 'em.

MISS RONBERRY

So am I. They're so big. And so black. . . .

(SARAH *runs in, excited, leaving the door open behind her.*)

SARAH

A letter from the gentleman that own the barn. I had a good look at the seal!

MISS MOFFAT

At last . . .

MISS RONBERRY

What does it say?

MISS MOFFAT

Sir Herbert still cannot give a definite decision until the seventeenth. Another week wasted. This is infuriating.

MISS RONBERRY

Does it mean he may not let you have it?

SARAH

Oh. . . .

MISS MOFFAT

He must—it would ruin everything. . . .

MISS RONBERRY

Sarah—isn't there another empty building *anywhere* round here?

SARAH

There is the pigsties on the Maes Road, but they issn't big enough. (*She goes.*)

MISS RONBERRY

Oh, dear! Can't we start afresh somewhere else?

MISS MOFFAT

I've spent too much on preparations here—besides, I felt so right here from the start. . . . I *can't* leave now . . . I'm a Christian woman, but I could smack Sir Herbert's face till my arm dropped off.

(*The front door is opened unceremoniously and the* SQUIRE *strides in; he is in full evening dress.*)

47

THE SQUIRE

Jolly good evenin', teacher. Remember me?

MISS MOFFAT

Would you mind going outside, knocking, and waiting quite a long time before I say "Come in"?

THE SQUIRE

Jolly good! Parlor games, what?

MISS RONBERRY

But, Miss Moffat, it's the *Squire!* Squire, you must forget you ever saw me in this dress . .   So ashamed . . . I shan't be a moment . . . (*She runs upstairs into the bedroom.*)

THE SQUIRE

Rat tat tat, one two three four come in, one two three four, forward *march!* My dear madam, you're not in class now! (*A knock at the garden door*) Come in!

(ROBBART *and* MORGAN *enter from garden.* MORGAN *has lantern.*)

ROBBART

Please, Miss, for the bell.

THE SQUIRE

Evening, boys! (*Enter* JONES) Evening, Jones. I am appalled to observe, my boys, that you are still soiling your fingers in that disgusting coal mine!

MR. JONES

Excuse me, please. . . . (*He goes into the study.*)

THE SQUIRE

What's that you've got there?

ROBBART

Bell, syr, for the school.

THE SQUIRE

Up with it, boys, up with it! (ROBBART *lifts the crate and carries it out of the garden door, which* MORGAN *has opened for him.* MORGAN *follows him, shutting the door*) Ding dong bell—teacher's in the well! . . . Now, my dear madam—

MISS MOFFAT

I'm rather irritable this evening, so unless there's a reason for your visit . . .

THE SQUIRE

Oh, but there is! Very important message. Word of mouth. From a gent that's just been dining with me. Sir Herbert Vezey.

MISS MOFFAT

Yes? Oh, do be quick! . . .

THE SQUIRE

He has definitely decided that he has no use for the barn— but he does not see it as a school, and under no circumstances will he let it as such, so he must regretfully decline, et cetera.

49

MISS MOFFAT

(*Trying to hide her chagrin*)

He implied in his first letter that he would be willing to sell.

THE SQUIRE

Then some bigwig must have made him change his mind, mustn't he?

MISS MOFFAT

(*Suddenly looking at him, incredulously*)

You?

THE SQUIRE

(*Rising, serious, taking the floor with a certain authority*)

I have not called on you, madam, because I have been eyeing your activities very closely from afar. . . . It is with dis—disapproval and—er—dis—

MISS MOFFAT

It is unwise to embark on a speech with the vocabulary of a child of five.

THE SQUIRE

(*Suddenly aggressive*)

I am not going to have any of this damned hanky-panky in my village!

MISS MOFFAT

Your village!

THE SQUIRE

My village! I am no braggart, but I'd have you know that everything you can see from that window—and you haven't got a bad view—*I own!* Now, my dear madam . . .

MISS MOFFAT

(*In an outburst*)

And stop calling me your dear madam. I'm not married, I'm not French, and you haven't the slightest affection for me!

THE SQUIRE

Oh. . . . First of all, I'm not one to hit a woman below the belt. If you know what I mean. Always be fair—to the fair sex. . . . All my life I've done my level best for the villagers. They call me Squire, y'know, term of affection, jolly touching. . . . I mean, a hamper every Christmas, the whole shoot, and a whopping tankard of beer on my birthday, and on my twenty-firster they all got a mug . . .

MISS MOFFAT

Go on.

THE SQUIRE

They jabber away in that funny lingo, but bless their hearts, it's a free country! But puttin' 'em up to read English, and pothooks, and givin' 'em ideas . . . If there were more people like you, y'know, England'd be a jolly dangerous place to live in! What d'ye want to do, turn 'em into gentlemen? What's the idea?

MISS MOFFAT

I am beginning to wonder myself.

THE SQUIRE

Anyway, this buyin' 'em out of the mine is a lot of gammon. I own a half share in it.

51

MISS MOFFAT

That explains a good deal.

THE SQUIRE

Why don't you take up croquet? Keep you out of mischief.
(MISS RONBERRY *comes out of the bedroom*) Well, dear lady,
anything I can do to make your stay here a happier one . . .

MISS MOFFAT

Thank you.

THE SQUIRE

I must be getting back. If I know Sir Herbert, my best old
port will be no more . . .

MISS MOFFAT

Wait a minute.

THE SQUIRE

Yes?

MISS MOFFAT

I know I shall be sticking a pin into a whale, but here are
just two words about yourself. You are the Squire Bountiful,
are you? Adored by his contented subjects, intelligent and
benignly understanding, are you? I should just like to point
out that there is a considerable amount of dirt, ignorance,
misery and discontent abroad in this world, and that a good
deal of it is due to people like you, because you are a stupid,
conceited, greedy, good-for-nothing, addle-headed nincompoop, and you can go to blue blazes. Good night! (*She turns
away. A frozen pause.*)

52

THE CORN IS GREEN

THE SQUIRE

I perceive that you have been drinking. (*He goes.*)

(MISS RONBERRY *comes downstairs.*)

MISS MOFFAT

That was undignified, but I feel better for it. (*She sits on the bench, intensely depressed.*)

MISS RONBERRY

I am glad, because it *was* plain-spoken, wasn't it? Has he been nasty? So unlike the Squire . . .

MISS MOFFAT

He was kindness itself. He advised me to go and live in a hole in the ground with my knitting. He has persuaded the owner not to sell.

MISS RONBERRY

Oh, dear . . . of course . . . I always think men know best, don't you?

MISS MOFFAT

Yes.

MISS RONBERRY

I'm wearing my mousseline de soie, and he never even noticed. . . . What will you do?

MISS MOFFAT

Sell the house; take this brain child of a ridiculous spinster, and smother it. Have you got a handkerchief?

53

MISS RONBERRY

Yes, Miss Moffat. Why?

MISS MOFFAT

I want to blow my nose. (*She holds her hand out;* MISS RONBERRY *hands her the handkerchief. She blows her nose, and returns the handkerchief.*)

MISS RONBERRY

You ought to have had a cry. I love a cry when I'm depressed. Such an advantage over the gentlemen, I always think.

MISS MOFFAT
(*Opening the study door*)

Mr. Jones . . .

JONES
(*Off stage*)

Yes . . .

MISS MOFFAT

Will you write letters to the tradespeople and the mine? We are giving up the school . . .

JONES
(*Off stage*)

Oh!

MISS MOFFAT

I suppose we'd better start putting some order into this chaos, and get the business over . . . What are these filthy exercise books doing among my papers . . . ?

MISS RONBERRY

Those hooligans just now. They said Mr. Jones had picked them out because they could write English and would I mind my own some-dreadful-word business.

MISS MOFFAT

I set them an essay on "How I would spend my holiday." I must have been mad . . . (*Throws one book away and takes one from* MISS RONBERRY)

MISS RONBERRY
(*Reading, laboriously*)

"If—I has ever holiday—I has breakfast and talks then dinner and a rest, tea then nothing—then supper then I talk and I go sleep."

MISS MOFFAT

From exhaustion, I suppose. (BESSIE *comes in from the kitchen, gets hat from table and starts for door*) Where are you going?

BESSIE

Just another walk, Miss Moffat.

MISS RONBERRY

What's the matter, little dear?

BESSIE

Mum's hit me.

MISS RONBERRY

Oh, naughty mum. Why ?

55

BESSIE

Just because I told her she was common. (*She goes out.*)

MISS RONBERRY

That child *is* unhappy.

MISS MOFFAT

I can't be bothered with her. Another time I'd have been faintly amused by this one's idea of a holiday, judging by a rather crude drawing.

MISS RONBERRY

What is it?

MISS MOFFAT

A bicycling tour with me in bloomers.

MISS RONBERRY

Tch, tch . . .

MISS MOFFAT
(*Reading*)

" 'Holiday-time.' That carefree magic word! What shall it be this year, tobogganing among the eternal snows or tasting the joys of Father Neptune?"

MISS RONBERRY

But that's beautiful! Extraordinary!

MISS MOFFAT

I might think so too if I hadn't seen it in a book open on that desk. (*Throws book in wastebasket.*)

MISS RONBERRY

Oh!

MISS MOFFAT

No, your Squire was right. . . . I have been a stupid and impractical ass, and I can't imagine how . . . (*Looks at name on book. She begins to read, slowly, with difficulty*) "The mine is dark . . . If a light come in the mine . . . the rivers in the mine will run fast with the voice of many women; the walls will fall in, and it will be the end of the world."

(MISS RONBERRY *is listening, inquiringly.* MORGAN *enters brusquely. He has made no attempt to wash, but now that he is alone he half-emerges as a truculent, arresting boy with, latent in him, a very strong personality which his immaturity and natural inclination make him shy to display.*)

MORGAN

We put up the bell, Miss.

MISS RONBERRY

Shhh—the garden . . . (MORGAN *moves sulkily toward the door*) Do go on . . .

MISS MOFFAT

(*Reading*)

". . . So the mine is dark. . . . But when I walk through the Tan—something—shaft, in the dark, I can touch with my hands the leaves on the trees, and underneath . . . where the corn is green." (*Looks at* MORGAN.)

MORGAN

Go on readin'.

MISS MOFFAT

(*Reading*)

". . . There is a wind in the shaft, not carbon monoxide
they talk about, it smell like the sea, only like as if the sea
had fresh flowers lying about . . . and that is my holiday."
(*She looks at the name on book.* MORGAN *starts off, turns
quickly as she speaks*) Are you Morgan Evans?

MORGAN

Yes, Miss.

MISS MOFFAT

Did you write this?

MORGAN

(*After hesitation, sullenly*)

No, Miss.

MISS MOFFAT

But it's in your book.

MORGAN

Yes, Miss.

MISS MOFFAT

Then who wrote it?

MORGAN

I dunno, Miss.

(MISS MOFFAT *nods to* MISS RONBERRY, *who patters dis-
creetly into the study, closes door.*)

58

MISS MOFFAT

Did you write this? (*It is difficult to tell from the crisp severity of her manner that she is experiencing a growing inward excitement.* MORGAN *looks at her, distrustfully.*)

MORGAN

I dunno, Miss. . . . What iss the matter with it?

MISS MOFFAT

Sit down. (*He sits*) And take your cap off. (*He takes off his cap*) Spelling's deplorable, of course. "Mine" with two "n's," and "leaves" l, e, f, s.

MORGAN

What wass it by rights?

MISS MOFFAT

A "v," to start with.

MORGAN

I never 'eard o' no "v's," Miss.

MISS MOFFAT

Don't call me Miss.

MORGAN

Are you not a Miss?

MISS MOFFAT

Yes, I am, but it is not polite.

59

MORGAN

Oh.

MISS MOFFAT

You say "Yes, Miss Moffat," or "No, Miss Moffat." M, o, double f, a, t.

MORGAN

No "v's"?

MISS MOFFAT

No "v's." Where do you live?

MORGAN

Under the ground, Miss.

MISS MOFFAT

I mean your home.

MORGAN

Llyn-y-Mwyn, Miss . . . Moffat. Four miles from 'ere.

MISS MOFFAT

How big is it?

MORGAN

Four 'ouses and a beer-'ouse.

MISS MOFFAT

Have you any hobbies?

MORGAN

Oh, yes.

MISS MOFFAT

What?

MORGAN

Rum. (*He takes a small bottle of rum out of his pocket.*)

MISS MOFFAT

Rum? Do you live with your parents?

MORGAN

No, by my own self. My mother iss dead, and my father and my four big brothers wass in the Big Shaft Accident when I wass ten.

MISS MOFFAT

Killed?

MORGAN

Oh, yes, everybody wass.

MISS MOFFAT

What sort of man was your father?

MORGAN

'E was a mongrel.

MISS MOFFAT

A what?

MORGAN

'E had a dash of English. 'E learned it to me.

MISS MOFFAT

D'you go to chapel?

MORGAN

No, thank you.

MISS MOFFAT

Who taught you to read and write?

MORGAN

Tott?

MISS MOFFAT

Taught. The verb "to teach."

MORGAN

Oh, teached.

MISS MOFFAT

Who taught you?

MORGAN

I did.

MISS MOFFAT

Why?

MORGAN

I dunno.

MISS MOFFAT

What books have you read?

MORGAN

Books? A bit of the Bible and a book that a feller from the Plas kitchen nab for me.

MISS MOFFAT

What was it?

MORGAN

The Ladies' Companion! (MISS MOFFAT *rises and walks thoughtfully toward her desk, studying him. He sits uncom-*

fortably, twirling his cap between his fingers) Can I go now,
pliss . . .

MISS MOFFAT

No. (MORGAN *sits, taken aback*) Do you want to learn any
more?

MORGAN

No, thank you.

MISS MOFFAT

Why not?

MORGAN

The other men would have a good laugh.

MISS MOFFAT

I see. Have you ever written anything before this exercise?

MORGAN

No.

MISS MOFFAT

Why not?

MORGAN

Nobody never ask me to. What iss the matter with it?

MISS MOFFAT

Nothing's the matter with it. Whether it means anything
is too early for me to say, but it shows exceptional talent for
a boy in your circumstances.

MORGAN
(*Blinking and hesitating*)
Terrible long words, Miss Moffat.

63

MISS MOFFAT

This shows that you are very clever.
(*A pause. He looks up slowly, not sure if he has heard aright, looks at her searchingly, then away again. His mind is working uncertainly, but swiftly.*)

MORGAN

Oh.

MISS MOFFAT

Have you ever been told that before?

MORGAN

It iss news to me.

MISS MOFFAT

What effect does the news have on you?

MORGAN

It iss a bit sudden. It makes me that I . . . (*Hesitating, then plunging*) I want to get more clever still. I want to know what iss—behind of all them books. . . .

MISS MOFFAT

Miss Ronberry . . . (*To him*) Can you come tomorrow?

MORGAN

(*Taken by surprise*)
Tomorrow—no—I am workin' on the six-till-four shift.

MISS MOFFAT

Then can you be here at five?

64

MORGAN

Five—no, not before seven, Miss—six miles to walk . . .

MISS MOFFAT

Oh, yes, of course—seven then. In the meantime I'll correct this for spelling and grammar.

MORGAN

(*Staring at her, fascinated*)

Yes, Miss Moffat.

MISS MOFFAT

That will be all. Good night.

MORGAN

Good night, Miss Moffat.

MISS MOFFAT

Are you the one I spanked? (*He turns at the door, looks at her, smiles, blinks and goes*) Miss Ronberry! Mr. Jones!

(MISS RONBERRY *runs in from the study.*)

MISS RONBERRY

Yes?

MISS MOFFAT

I have been a deuce of a fool. It doesn't matter about the barn; we are going to start the school, in a small way at first, in this room. . . . And I am going to get those youngsters out of that mine if I have to black my face and go down and fetch them myself! Get Jonesy before he posts those letters, and tell those others I'll be ready for them in five minutes. We are going on with the school! (MISS RONBERRY *scampers into the study, rather dazed. Her voice is heard, calling: "We are going on with the school!" The door shuts behind her.* MISS MOFFAT *reads from the exercise book*) ". . . and when I walk—in the dark . . . I can touch with my hands . . . where the corn is green. . . ."

(*The school bell rings*)

Curtain

ACT TWO

ACT TWO

An early evening in August, two years later; the sun is still bright.

The room is now a complete jumble of living room and schoolroom, and there is every sign of cheerful overcrowding. The table in the window recess is replaced by a double school desk; the table and its small chair are pushed behind the sofa; a school desk stands isolated between the big open-top desk and the sofa; between the sofa and the bay window, two rows of four school desks each, squeezed together and facing the audience at an angle. Charts, maps, an alphabet list are pinned up higgledy-piggledy over all the books; a large world globe on the shelf; hat-pegs have been fixed irregularly back of right door above and below kitchen door. Books overflow everywhere, all over the dresser especially, in place of plates; the hat-pegs are loaded with caps and hats; MISS MOFFAT's cloak hangs on a hook on the back of the front door; a blackboard lies on the sofa upside down, with "Constantinople is the capital of Turkey" written across in MISS RONBERRY's tremulous handwriting. The lamp on the table has been removed. Potted plants on the window sills.

Before the curtain rises, voices are heard singing, in harmony, in Welsh, "Bugeilio'r Gwenyth Gwyn"; children, shrill, sweet and self-confident, reinforced by harmony from older boys and parents, especially SARAH.

The room seems full of people; MISS RONBERRY stands

69

perched on the tiny stool between the sofa and the foot of the stairs, her back to the audience, conducting stiffly; MR. JONES *is crouched in the desk chair, correcting exercises at the open desk.* SARAH, *two older peasant women in shawls, and three older men in their shabby best stand crowded behind the eight desks and in the window recess. In the front row of desks sit* ROBBART, IDWAL, *a little girl, and* GLYN THOMAS; *in the second sit another little boy, another little girl,* BESSIE *and* WILL HUGHES. *In another desk pushed provisionally next the front row sits* JOHN OWEN, *and in the other isolated one sits* OLD TOM, *an elderly distinguished-looking peasant, his cap and stick before him, carried away by the music. A young girl sits at table.*

BESSIE *is silent, bored, and prettier than ever, though still dressed as a sober little schoolgirl. The boys we saw before as miners are clean and almost spruce; the parents follow every movement of* MISS RONBERRY'S *with avid curiosity. The pupils have slates and slate pencils in front of them.*

The song is sung through to the end.

MISS RONBERRY

Now that was quite better. Full of splendid feeling, and nice and precise as well. Have you all got my English translation? (*She climbs down from her stool.*)

THE PUPILS

Yes, Miss Ronberry.

MISS RONBERRY

Are you all quite sure of the meaning of "Thou lovedest him, fair maid, that doth not love thee back?"

(*Four older people follow with motion of lips.*)

THE PUPILS

Yes, Miss Ronberry.

(*Four people speak the line after the others have said it.*)

OLD TOM
(*Singing stentoriously, in broken English*)
"That doth not luff thee . . . ba-a-ck!"

MISS RONBERRY

Capital, Mr. Tom. (*She takes a small handbell from a hook beneath the stairs, rings it vigorously, and hangs it up again; nobody moves*) Home sweet home, children! Boys and girls, come out to play!

(MISS PUGH *nudges* IDWAL.)

IDWAL

Please, Miss Ronberry, can we have some more?

MISS RONBERRY

Well, just the tiniest lesson. We must keep to the curriculum. (*Steps upon stool again*) Now what would you like?

IDWAL

Please, Miss Ronberry, how do you spell it?

MISS RONBERRY

What, dear?

71

OLD TOM

Curriculum!

MISS RONBERRY

What would you like? The rivers of Europe or King Alfred and the cakes?

OLD TOM

Multiplication table!

(*Some say "Yes." Others repeat "multiplications."*)

MISS RONBERRY

Well, twice six are twelve!

(*One old man does not recite. He smiles.*)

THE PUPILS

Twice seven are fourteen—twice eight are sixteen—
    (*They complete the table.*)

OLD TOM

Twice thirteen are twenty-six!

MISS RONBERRY

Capital—school dismiss!

(IDWAL *crosses front of desk to window. All rise except*
    BESSIE.)

GLYN THOMAS

Be'di'r gloch, Merry?

IST GIRL

Chwarter i bump.

A MOTHER

What iss the next thing in the multiplication?

A BOY

Wn i ddim yn wyr—gofyn iddi— (*Rises.*)

A MOTHER

Why issn't there any geography now?

SARAH PUGH

Friday geography, Thursday today . . .

AN OLD LADY

Pnawn dydd Iau, te, hanner awr wedi tri—

IDWAL

Dyma'r fistress!

(MISS MOFFAT *walks in from the garden. All rise but*
BESSIE *She is more alert and businesslike than ever.*
She is studying an exercise book. She goes into the
kitchen.)

SARAH PUGH

Miss Moffat.

A YOUNG FATHER

Oh, yes.

SARAH PUGH

Mi ddylaswn fod yn pobi heddyw—
A dwidi gadal y cig yn y popdy—

73

A MOTHER

Mi fydd eich cegin chi ar dan, Mrs. Pugh—

IDWAL

'Nhad, gai fynd i chwara yn nghae John Davies—

A FATHER

(*Answering him*)

Ddim heddyw—dwisho ti gartre—

1ST GIRL

Yforty d'wi am drio sgwennu llythyr— (*Crossing to* 2ND GIRL.)

2ND GIRL

Os gynnachi steel-pen golew?

WILL HUGHES

Mae'na gymaint o flots!

3RD GIRL

Dwi wedi sgwennu llythyr at fy nain, wni ddim be ddidi'thi.

WILL HUGHES

Welsochi 'rioed eiriau fel one?

SARAH PUGH

Fedri'thi ddim canu fel Cymraes, digon siwr—

ROBBART ROBBATCH

Mae'r hen ddyn am ofyn rwbeth iddi eto—drychwch arno—

74

SARAH PUGH

Mi gollith'o ei Gymraeg cyn bo hir—
Idwal, what you looking so sorry—always wanting to know something—

3RD GIRL

Mae genni just ddigon o amswer i gyrraedd at y llyn—
Mae'r dwr yn rhy oer i ymdrochi—

SARAH PUGH

Nag ydi—mae'r haul wedı bod yn rhy boeth heddyw—

(*The crowd finally trickle out, shepherded by* MISS RONBERRY. *Besides* BESSIE, *there are left* OLD TOM, *studying,* MISS RONBERRY *and* IDWAL.)

IDWAL

Miss Ronberry, please, what is four times fourteen?

MISS RONBERRY

Thank you so much for the flowers, Idwal, dear.

IDWAL

Yes, Miss Ronberry. (*He follows the others; leaves door open.*)

MISS RONBERRY

Is there anything you would like to know, Mr. Tom?

OLD TOM

Where iss Shakespeare?

MISS RONBERRY

Where? Shakespeare, Mr. Tom, was a very great writer.

75

OLD TOM

Writer? Like the Beibl?

MISS RONBERRY

Like the Bible.

OLD TOM

Dear me, and me thinkin' the man was a place. (*Following the others, muttering sadly*) If I iss been born fifty years later, I iss been top of the class.

MISS RONBERRY

Oh, dear . . . (*Tidying the desks.* BESSIE *crawls over seats to small desk*) Miss Moffat has been doing grammar with Form Two under the pear tree for an hour, she must be dead. . . . Why did you not get up when she crossed? (*She takes a pumice stone from a drawer.*)

BESSIE

My foot went to sleep. (*Her manner is more impudent than ever.*)

MISS RONBERRY

That, dear, is a naughty fib.

BESSIE

(*Sits*)

If you want to know, Miss Ronberry, I feel quite faint sometimes, as if my heart'd stopped and the world was coming to an end.

MISS RONBERRY

(*With guileless solicitude*)

Bessie, dear, how *horrid!*

MR. JONES

It may be in the nature of a premonition.

MISS RONBERRY

A what?

MR. JONES

I had a premonition once. Like a wave of the ocean breakin' on a sea shell. Something had said to me that mornin': "Walk, and think, and keep off the food, for thirteen hours." So I ordered my supper, and I went. Towards the end of the day (MISS MOFFAT *enters from kitchen*) I was sittin' on a stile in a cloak of meditation; and a voice roared at me: "John Goronwy Jones, tomorrow morning is the end of the world!"

MISS MOFFAT

And was it?

MR. JONES
(*Sadly*)

It was eight years ago. It was a splendid experience.

MISS MOFFAT

Which proves how much the gift of prophecy can owe to an empty stomach. . . . Anybody seen a Greek book? (*Picking up a tiny volume*) Here it is . . . (*Starting toward stairs.*)

MISS RONBERRY

Greek, Miss Moffat?

MISS MOFFAT

Morgan Evans is starting Greek this month.

MISS RONBERRY

No! I didn't know you knew Greek?

MISS MOFFAT

I don't; I've just got to keep one day ahead of him and trust to luck. (*She disappears into her bedroom.*)

MISS RONBERRY

To think that two years ago he hardly knew English!

BESSIE

Stuck-up teacher's pet.

MISS RONBERRY

You must not think that, dear, Miss Moffat says he is clever.

BESSIE

He always looks right through me, so I don't know, I'm sure. Stuck-up teacher's pet. . . . I got some scent on my hands, Mr. Jones, like to smell them?

MR. JONES

No, thank you, Bessie, I can smell them from here, thank you.

BESSIE

(*Sniffing her hands, softly*)

Ooh, it's lovely. . . .

MISS RONBERRY

She has some wonderful plans for him—I can tell by her manner. I think she is trying to send him to one of those

Church schools so that he can get a curateship. Would not that be exciting?

BESSIE

(Indolently)

I think she's ridin' for a fall.

(JONES *turns, looks, and goes back to his work.*)

MISS RONBERRY

Bessie! Why?

BESSIE

All this orderin' 'im about. I've got eyes in my head, if she hasn't, and he's gettin' sick of it. I think a lady ought to be dainty. She's no idea.

(MISS MOFFAT *appears at the top of the stairs.*)

MISS MOFFAT

Evans! (*A pause.* MORGAN *comes in from the study. He is now seventeen. He is dressed in a shabby country suit, and is at the moment the submissive schoolboy, very different from the first act. He carries a sheet of writing and a pen.* MISS MOFFAT'S *attitude to him seems purely impersonal. The others watch them*) Finished?

MORGAN

Yes, Miss Moffat.

(MISS RONBERRY *rubs ink off her hands with pumice stone.*)

79

MISS MOFFAT

How many pages?

MORGAN

Nine.

MISS MOFFAT

Three too many. Boil down to six. Have you got those lines of Voltaire?

MORGAN

Yes, Miss Moffat.

MISS MOFFAT

It's just five—have your walk now, good and brisk. . . .

(MORGAN, *taking his cap from a peg, starts for the front door.*)

MORGAN

Yes, Miss Moffat. (*Stops.*)

MISS MOFFAT

But kill two birds and get the Voltaire by heart. If you can ever argue a point like that, you'll do. Back in twenty minutes—and take your pen from behind your ear. (*She disappears into her bedroom. Her manner is too matter of fact to be unkind, but* MORGAN *is not taking it well. He throws his pen on to a desk.*)

BESSIE

Now turn a somersault and beg. (*He looks at her with contempt. She returns his stare brazenly. She turns to see if the others are noticing.* MISS RONBERRY *is busy with her pumice stone and* MR. JONES *is engrossed in his work.* BESSIE

looks away from them all, suddenly soft and mysterious)
Can you smell scent?

MORGAN

Yes.

BESSIE
(*Dreamily*)

Nice, isn't it?

MORGAN

I don't know, I never come across scent before. (*Correcting himself unwillingly*) I did never come across—scent before. . . .

BESSIE

Bright, aren't you? Don't you ever get tired of lessons? (JONES *looks in disapproval. She begins to sing "With His Bell Bottom Trousers." He goes to the front door, turns, then goes, banging the door. She flings down her slate*) There we go. And my mummy ought to be back soon, and then we'll know somethin'.

MR. JONES
What is the matter? Where has she gone?

BESSIE
One of her prayer meetings. Twenty miles to shake a tambourine in the open air. I think it's wicked. . . . She ought to be just in time, and then we'll know.

MR. JONES

Know what?

BESSIE

About that horrid Morgan Evans. It's been lessons every night with teacher, hasn't it, since we left the mine? And long walks in between, to blow the cobwebs away? But the last week or two we've been breaking our journey, so we've heard.

MR. JONES

How do you mean?

BESSIE

A glass of rum next door at the Gwesmor Arms and then another, and then another!

MR. JONES
(*Perturbed*)
Oh. . . . Whoever told you that?

BESSIE

A little bird. And if my mummy's sciatica's better she's going to jump up and look over the frosty part, and then we'll *know*.

(MRS. WATTY *hurries in through the front door, in high spirits. She wears an ill-fitting Militant Righteousness Corps uniform, and carries an umbrella and a brown-paper parcel.*)

MRS. WATTY

Guess what's 'appened to me!

BESSIE

What?

MRS. WATTY

I'm a Sergeant-Major!

(MISS MOFFAT *has come out on to the landing; her hair is down and she is brushing it.*)

MISS MOFFAT

Watty, you're not!

(JONES *turns to* MISS MOFFAT.)

MRS. WATTY

Oh, ma'am, I didn't see you . . .

MISS MOFFAT

Tell me more!

MRS. WATTY

You remember Sergeant-Major 'Opkins desertin' in Cardiff and marryin' a sailor?

MISS MOFFAT

Yes?

MRS. WATTY

Well, last week, not two months after she give up the Corpse, she was dead!

MISS MOFFAT

And you've stepped into her shoes?

MRS. WATTY

They're a bit on the big side; but I can put a bit of paper

in. The uniform fits lovely, though. I'll get you a cup o' tea and an egg, ma'am, you never 'ad that cold meat, ma'am, I'll be bound?

MISS MOFFAT

Folk eat too much anyway. (*She goes back into her bedroom.*)

BESSIE

Did you jump?

MRS. WATTY
(*Coming back into the room*)
Just caught 'im. (*To* MR. JONES, *sorrowfully*) He was 'avin' a good drink, sir. . . . (*To* BESSIE) Don't you dare tell 'er, you little dollymop, or I'll rattle your bones. . . .

(MISS MOFFAT *reappears and comes downstairs.*)

MISS MOFFAT
Was it a nice service, Watty?

MRS. WATTY
Beautiful, ma'am. They said they 'oped the late Sergeant-Major was gone where we all want to go, but with 'er having deserted they couldn't be sure. Then we saved three sinners. You ought to been there. . . . And the collection! (*Starts for kitchen*) I 'adn't seed so much oof since the Great Liverpool Exhibition.

MISS RONBERRY
But they didn't make a collection at the Liverpool Exhibition, did they?

84

MRS. WATTY

No, but I did.

(MR. JONES *takes blackboard to settle.* MISS RONBERRY *gets book from dresser.* MRS. WATTY *goes to kitchen.*)

BESSIE

Please, Miss Moffat, can I have the money for my ticket?

(MR. JONES *draws diagram on blackboard.*)

MISS MOFFAT

What ticket?

BESSIE

For Tregarna Fair tomorrow. You said I could go.

MISS MOFFAT

On the contrary, I said you couldn't. Not in school hours.

MISS RONBERRY

Are you feeling better, dear?

BESSIE

No, Miss Ronberry. It's all this sittin' down. It's been going on for two years now. I heard tell it ends in everythin' rottin' away.

MISS MOFFAT

(*Sitting at desk*)

What's rotting away?

85

MISS RONBERRY

Bessie says she's been sitting down for two years.

MISS MOFFAT

She's lucky. My feet feel as if I've been standing for the same length of time. What are these, Ron?

MISS RONBERRY·

Two more accounts, I fear.

MISS MOFFAT

Oh, yes. The Liddell and Scott and Evans's new suit. Tch . . . (*Cheerfully*) I shall have to sell out a couple more shares, I expect.

MISS RONBERRY

Oh, dear.

MISS MOFFAT

Not at all. It's easy to squander money, and it's easy to hoard it. The most difficult thing in the world is to use it. And if I've learned to use it, I've *done* something. That's better. . . . My plans are laid, Ron, my dear, my plans are laid! But don't ask me what I'm hatching, because I can't tell you till tomorrow.

MISS RONBERRY

You are wonderful!

MISS MOFFAT

Go to Halifax. (MISS RONBERRY *sits on couch and studies from book*) I'm enjoying myself. (*Huge sigh from* BESSIE) Bessie Watty, what is this dying duck business?

BESSIE

Yes, Miss Moffat.

MISS MOFFAT

Don't "yes, Miss Moffat" me. Explain yourself.

BESSIE

My mummy said all these lessons is bad for my inside.

MISS MOFFAT

She told me they stop you eating sweets, but perhaps I am telling the lie.

BESSIE

Yes, Miss Moffat.

MISS MOFFAT

What's the matter with your inside?

BESSIE

It goes round and round through sittin' down. P'r'aps what I want is a change.

MISS MOFFAT

(*Muttering*)

"Adelphos, a brother" . . . There is nothing to prevent you going for walks between lessons. You can go for one now, as far as Sarah Pugh Postman, to see if my new chalks have arrived. (*Looking at* BESSIE, *as the latter stares before her without moving*) Quick march.

BESSIE

I'm not goin'.

MISS MOFFAT

What did you say?

BESSIE

I'm not goin'. Everybody's against me. . . . I'm goin' to throw myself off of a cliff, an' kill myself. . . . It'll make a nice case in the papers, me in pieces at the bottom of a cliff! I'm goin' mad, mad, and I'm goin' to kill myself, nothin' goin' to stop me—stone dead at the bottom of a cliff—ah—ah—ah . . .

(MRS. WATTY *strides in from the kitchen with a cupful of cold water which she throws into her daughter's face.*)

MRS. WATTY

(*To* MISS MOFFAT)

I made a mess o' your rug, ma'am, but it's worth it. She's got bad blood, this girl, mark my word.

MISS RONBERRY

She'll catch her death!

MRS. WATTY

Nothing like cold water, ma'am. I learnt that with her father. 'E was foreign, you know. (*She goes back into the kitchen.* MISS MOFFAT *studies* BESSIE *with distaste.*)

MISS MOFFAT

And how do you feel after that?

BESSIE

I can't remember anything. I'm in a comma.

MISS MOFFAT

(*Taking her by the arm, starts pushing her upstairs*)

We'll sit on our bed for an hour with the door locked, shall we, and *try* to remember? And next week you go away into service and see how we like that. . . . (*She pushes her out of sight into the passage; a door bangs; the noise of a lock turning.* MISS MOFFAT *comes downstairs, tucking the key into her petticoat pocket*) I must count her as one of my failures. Fish out of water, of course. Guttersnipe species—if there is such a fish. She'll be more at home in service. . . . (*Muttering*) "Dendron, a tree—"

MISS RONBERRY

I beg your pardon . . . ? Oh, Miss Moffat, I am bursting with curiosity—your plans for Morgan Evans—is it a curateship?

MISS MOFFAT

(*Slowly, amused*)

No, it isn't a curateship. (*She laughs happily, walks toward the desk and takes up an exercise book.*)

MISS RONBERRY

I really don't see anything funny about curates. (*To* MR. JONES) I mean, there is nothing *wrong* with curates, is there?

MR. JONES

No, except that they ought to go to chapel.

MISS MOFFAT

Who has been writing in here?

THE CORN IS GREEN

(MRS. WATTY *appears at the kitchen door.*)

MRS. WATTY

Your egg, ma'am!

MISS MOFFAT

"Bessie Watty has the face of an angel!"

(JONES *takes hat from peg, goes to door.*)

MISS RONBERRY

What an extraordinary . . .

MISS MOFFAT

But I know the writing. John Goronwy Jones, I'm ashamed
of you.

MR. JONES

I shall see you tomorrow if we are spared.

MISS RONBERRY
(*Shocked*)

Oh!

MR. JONES

You all misjudge that little girl. She has the face of a good
woman in the melting pot.

MISS MOFFAT

I've got the face of a good woman, too, and well out of the
melting pot, but I don't think I'd ever find it in writing. (*She
goes into the kitchen.*)

90

MRS. WATTY

I never thought I'd live to call *you* a naughty old man. (*She follows* MISS MOFFAT *into the kitchen.* MR. JONES *goes out through the front door.* MISS RONBERRY *gets her hat and shawl and crosses to small mirror in bookcase. The front door opens abruptly and* MORGAN *appears. He is dishevelled, and it is fairly apparent that he has been drinking. His manner is defiant. The door bangs behind him.*)

MISS RONBERRY

Oh, it's you, Morgan. . . . (*Back at the mirror*) Miss Moffat is having something to eat.

MORGAN

And I have been having something to drink, so we are quits.

MISS RONBERRY

(*Looking at him sharply, the unpleasant truth dawning on her*)

I will tell her that you are back. . . .

MORGAN

I don't want to see no Miss Moffat.

MISS RONBERRY

You mean "I don't want to see Miss Moffat." The double negative. . . .

MORGAN

Now don't you start! . . . I like the double negative, it says what I want the way I like, and I am *not* goin' to stand *no*

91

interferences from *nobody!* Voltaire indeed ... (*Crumples paper, kicks it savagely into a corner.*)

MISS RONBERRY

Morgan! I've never seen you like this before!

MORGAN

You haven't, have you? (*In a rising torrent of invective*) Well, now I come to think of it, I haven't neither, not for two years, and I'm surprised by meself, and shocked by meself! 'Goin' inside one o' them public houses and puttin' me nice clean boots on that dirty rail, and me dainty lady fingers on that detestable mucky counter! Pourin' poison rum down me nice clean teeth, and spittin' in a spittoon. What's come over you, Morgan Evans? You come back to your little cage, and if you comb hair and wash hands and get your grammar right and forget you was once the Middle-weight Champion of the Glasynglo Miners, we might give you a nice bit of sewin' to do ... Where's that Bessie Watty, sendin' her mother to spy on me, I'll knock her bloody block off. ...

MISS RONBERRY

(*Outraged*)

Morgan Evans, *language!* Don't you dare use an expression like that to me again!

MORGAN

(*Facing her, leaning over couch*)

I got plenty of others, thank you, and they are all comin' out. I am goin' to surprise quite a few ...

(MISS MOFFAT *enters from the kitchen.*)

92

MISS MOFFAT

Have a good walk, Evans?

MORGAN

Yes, Miss Moffat.

MISS MOFFAT

Can you repeat the Voltaire? (*Sitting on the sofa, drinking milk.*)

MORGAN

Not yet.

MISS MOFFAT

It's very short.

MORGAN

Paper blowed away.

MISS MOFFAT

Oh. Copy it again, will you, and bring it to me.

MORGAN
(*Muttering*)

Yes, Miss Moffat.

MISS MOFFAT
(*Holding out the jug*)

Would you like a drink?

(MORGAN *stops.*)

MORGAN

No, thank you. (*He goes into the study.*)

93

MISS MOFFAT

I hope he's not going to be slow at French. It'll make the Greek so much more difficult. . . .

MISS RONBERRY

You don't think perhaps all this—in his situation—is rather sudden for him? I mean . . .

MISS MOFFAT

Not for him, my dear. He has the most brilliantly receptive brain I've ever come across. Don't tell him so, but he has.

MISS RONBERRY

I know his *brain* is all right. . . .

MISS MOFFAT

I'm very pleased with his progress, on the whole. . . . (*A knock at the front door.* MISS RONBERRY *moves toward the door.* MISS MOFFAT *stops her*) Wait a minute! (*Crosses to alcove window. Peering out toward the front door*) Yes, it is. . . .

MISS RONBERRY

Who?

MISS MOFFAT

Royalty, the Conservatives and all the Grand Lamas rolled into one. The Squire.

MISS RONBERRY

The Squire! Oh, *my!*

MISS MOFFAT

It is indeed. Oh, my—let me have your shawl.

MISS RONBERRY

But he hasn't been here since that dreadful evening. . . .

MISS MOFFAT

I (*Going upstairs*) behaved more stupidly that night than I ever have in my life, and that's saying something. . . .

MISS RONBERRY

But why is he here now?

MISS MOFFAT

Never you mind. . . . All I can tell you is that it is to do with Morgan Evans, and that it is vital I make the right impression.

MISS RONBERRY
(*As* MISS MOFFAT *runs upstairs*)
What sort of impression?

MISS MOFFAT
(*On last step*)
Helpless and clinging, or as near as dammit . . .
(*She disappears into her room, as there is a second impatient knock at the front door.*)

MISS RONBERRY

Come in!

(*The door opens and the* GROOM *appears.*)

THE CORN IS GREEN

THE GROOM
(*Announcing*)

The Squire.

(*The* SQUIRE *follows the* GROOM, *who retires and shuts the door.*)

THE SQUIRE

Good afternoon. (*He is dressed in a summer lounge suit, and holds his hat in his hand.*)

MISS RONBERRY

Your hat, Squire . . .

THE SQUIRE

No, thank you, I am not staying.

MISS RONBERRY

Oh, dear, I do look a sketch . . .

THE SQUIRE
(*Looks around*)

So this is the seat of learning.

MISS RONBERRY

We are always on the point of a good spring-clean. How dreadful that we have no refreshment to offer you!

THE SQUIRE

You can tell her from me that I am not here to be insulted again.

MISS RONBERRY

Oh, I'm sure you aren't! I mean . . .

THE SQUIRE

She called me an addle-headed nincompoop.

(MISS MOFFAT *comes downstairs, a lace shawl draped over her shoulder. She carries a bowl of flowers.*)

MISS MOFFAT

Miss Ronberry, dear, my roses are dying. . . . Would you pour out a little water for them, I have such a headache I don't think . . . (*Feigning surprise*) Squire!

THE SQUIRE

You wrote to me. Perhaps you have forgotten.

MISS MOFFAT

How could I forget! I only thought that after the overwrought fashion of my behaviour at our last meeting you must ignore my very nervous invitation. Miss Ronberry, a chair, dear, for the Squire. . . .

(*Startled,* MISS RONBERRY *takes a small chair from desk.*)

THE SQUIRE

I have not a great deal of time to spare, I fear.

MISS MOFFAT

Of course you haven't, I was just saying to Miss Ronberry, he's so busy he'll *never* be able to fit it in! Miss Ronberry,

97

dear, would you get some water for them? (*She hands the bowl to* MISS RONBERRY, *who passes the* SQUIRE *and goes into the garden bewildered*) Tell me, Squire, how did your prize-giving fare this afternoon?

THE SQUIRE

Rather a bore, y'know.

MISS MOFFAT

I had so hoped to see you judge. I love flowers.

THE SQUIRE

It wasn't flowers. It was cows.

MISS MOFFAT

Oh. It was your speech I wanted to hear, of course; I heard you made such an amusing one at the Croquet.

THE SQUIRE

Oh, did they tell you about that? Rather a good pun, eh? (*Laughing*) Ha, ha . . . I—may I sit down?

MISS MOFFAT

Do!

THE SQUIRE

I thought Griffith, the butcher, was going to laugh his napper off.

MISS MOFFAT

Indeed . . . Do you know, Squire, that makes me rather proud?

98

THE SQUIRE

Proud? Why?

MISS MOFFAT

Because he would not have understood a word if his little
girls hadn't learnt English at my school.

THE SQUIRE

Oh. Never thought of it like that. . . . (*As she puts her
hand to her head, says "Oh"*) Headache?

MISS MOFFAT

Squire, you see before you a tired woman. We live and
learn, and I have learnt how right you were that night. I
have worked my fingers to the bone battering my head against
a stone wall.

THE SQUIRE

But I heard you were a spiffing success.

MISS MOFFAT

Oh, no.

THE SQUIRE
(*Muttering*)
It's fair of you to admit it, I must say.

MISS MOFFAT

You see, in one's womanly enthusiasm one forgets that the
qualities vital to success in this sort of venture are completely
lacking in one: intelligence, courage and authority. . . . The
qualities, in short, of a man.

THE SQUIRE

Come, come, you mustn't be too hard on yourself, y'know. After all, you've meant well.

MISS MOFFAT

It's kind of you to say that.

THE SQUIRE

What about this Jones chappie?

MISS MOFFAT

He's a dear creature, but . . . I have no wish to be fulsome. I mean a man like yourself.

THE SQUIRE

I see.

MISS MOFFAT

One gets into such muddles! You'd never believe!

THE SQUIRE

Well . . . I've never been on your side, but I'm sorry to hear you've come a cropper. When are you giving it up?

MISS MOFFAT

Oh . . . That again is difficult; I have all my widow's mite, as it were, in the venture. . . .

(MORGAN *appears from the study carrying a paper. He has regained his self-control.*)

MORGAN

(*Stops*)

Please excuse me—

MISS MOFFAT

It's all right, Evans. Have you copied it? On my desk, will you?

MORGAN

Excuse me, sir . . . Good afternoon, sir.

THE SQUIRE

Good afternoon, my boy.

MORGAN

Excuse me, sir . . . Thank you. (*He goes.*)

THE SQUIRE

Nice well-spoken lad. Relative?

MISS MOFFAT

No. A pupil. He used to be one of your miners.

THE SQUIRE

No!

MISS MOFFAT

I'm glad you thought he was a nice well-spoken lad.

THE SQUIRE

Yes . . . One of my miners, interesting . . .

MISS MOFFAT

Because he is the problem I should like your advice about.

THE SQUIRE

What's he been up to, poaching?

MISS MOFFAT

No.

THE SQUIRE

A bit o' muslin?

MISS MOFFAT
(*Amused*)

No, no . . . There are none, anyway. . . .

THE SQUIRE
(*Suddenly shrewd*)

What about the little Cockney filly?

MISS MOFFAT

Bessie Watty? Oh, no, I assure you—she's a schoolgirl. . . .

THE SQUIRE

I dunno, all these young people growing up together, y'know—eh?

MISS MOFFAT

I think it's good for them . . . No, there's nothing of that sort—but he's a problem just the same. And like a true woman I have to scream for help to a man. To you.

THE SQUIRE
(*Completely won*)
Scream away, dear lady, scream away!

MISS MOFFAT
Well, he's—clever.

THE SQUIRE
Oh, is he? Good at figures, and all that? Because if he is, there's no reason why I shouldn't put him in my Mine Office, as junior office boy. What d'ye think of that?

MISS MOFFAT
No. Figures aren't his strong point.

THE SQUIRE
Thought you said he was clever.

MISS MOFFAT
To begin with, he can write.

THE SQUIRE
Oh. Well?

MISS MOFFAT
Very well.

THE SQUIRE
Then he could make fair copies. Eh?

MISS MOFFAT
No. (*Choosing her words carefully*) This boy——is quite out of the ordinary.

THE SQUIRE

Sure?

MISS MOFFAT

As sure as one of your miners would be, cutting through coal and striking a diamond without a flaw. He was born with very exceptional gifts. They must be—they ought to be given every chance.

THE SQUIRE

You mean he might turn into a literary bloke?

MISS MOFFAT

He might, yes.

THE SQUIRE

I'm blowed! How d'ye know?

MISS MOFFAT

By his work. It's very good.

THE SQUIRE

How d'ye know it's good?

MISS MOFFAT

How does one know Shakespeare's good?

THE SQUIRE

Shakespeare? What's he got to do with it?

MISS MOFFAT

He was a literary bloke.

THE SQUIRE

Ye-es. *He* was good, of course.

MISS MOFFAT

This little tenant of yours, Squire, has it in him to bring great credit to you.

THE SQUIRE

Yes, he *is* a tenant of mine, isn't he?

MISS MOFFAT

Imagine if you could say that you had known—well, say, Lord Tennyson, as a boy on your estate!

THE SQUIRE

Rather a lark, what? Though it's a bit different, y'know. Tennyson was at Cambridge. My old college.

MISS MOFFAT

Oh . . . Poor Evans. What a pity he was not born at the beginning of the eighteenth century!

THE SQUIRE

Beginning of the eighteenth century . . . Now when was that . . . ?

MISS MOFFAT

He would have had a protector. (*Takes two books from bookcase.*)

THE SQUIRE

What against?

MISS MOFFAT

A patron. Pope, you recall, dedicated the famous "Essay on Man" to his protector. (*Crosses front of small desk.*)

THE SQUIRE

"To H. St. John Lord Bolingbroke." Mmm . . . I *have* heard of it, now I remember. . . .

MISS MOFFAT

Isn't it wonderful to think that that inscription is handed down to posterity? (*Reading from the other book*) "To the Right Honourable Earl of Southampton . . . Your Honour's in all duty, William Shakespeare."

THE SQUIRE

Oh.

MISS MOFFAT

I often think of the pride that surged in the Earl's bosom when his encouragement gave birth to the masterpiece of a poor and humble writer!

THE SQUIRE

Funny, I never thought of Shakespeare being poor, somehow.

MISS MOFFAT

Some say his father was a butcher. The Earl realized he had genius, and fostered it.

THE SQUIRE

Mmm! If this boy really is clever, it seems a pity for *me* not to do something about it, doesn't it?

MISS MOFFAT

A great pity. And I can tell you exactly how you can do something about it.

THE SQUIRE

How?

MISS MOFFAT

There's a scholarship going.

THE SQUIRE

Scholarship? Where?

MISS MOFFAT

To Oxford.

THE SQUIRE
(*Staggered*)

Oxford?

MISS MOFFAT
(*Moves closer*)

A scholarship to Trinity College, Oxford, open to boys of secondary education in the British Isles. My school hardly comes under the heading of secondary education, and I wrote to your brother at Magdalen; he pulled some strings for me, and they have agreed to make a special case of this boy, on one condition. That you vouch for him. Will you?

THE SQUIRE

My dear lady, you take the cake . . . Can't he be just as clever at home?

MISS MOFFAT

No, he can't. For the sort of future he ought to have, he must have polish—he has everything else. The background of

a university would be invaluable to him. . . . (SQUIRE *rises*)
Will you?

THE SQUIRE

Well, the 'Varsity, y'know, hang it all . . . Mind you, he'll
never get it.

MISS MOFFAT

I know, but he *must* have the chance. . . .

THE SQUIRE

Still, y'know, even the mere prospect of one o' my miners . . .

MISS MOFFAT

Think of Shakespeare!

THE SQUIRE

All serene. (MISS MOFFAT *rises*) I'll drop a line to Henry
next week. Rather a lark, what? I must be off . . .

MISS MOFFAT

I should be most obliged if the letter could be posted tomorrow. Would you like me to draft out a recommendation
and send it over to the Hall? You must be so busy with the
estate. . . .

THE SQUIRE

I am rather. Polka supper tomorrow night . . . Yes, do do
that. Good-bye, dear lady!

MISS MOFFAT

Thank you so very much, Squire. . . .

THE SQUIRE

Happier conditions, and all that! Glad you've come to your senses!

MISS MOFFAT

Thank you so very much, Squire!

THE SQUIRE

Not at all, I'm all for giving a writer-fellow a helping hand. Tell my brother that, if you like . . . Good-bye—Good-bye. (*Exits.* MISS MOFFAT *closes door.* MISS RONBERRY *hurries in from the garden, carrying the bowl of roses. The afternoon sun begins to set.*)

MISS RONBERRY

Well? (*Puts vase on desk.*)

MISS MOFFAT

That man is so stupid it sits on him like a halo.

MISS RONBERRY

What happened?

MISS MOFFAT

In ten minutes I have given the Squire the impression that he spends his whole time fostering genius in the illiterate.

MISS RONBERRY

But how?

MISS MOFFAT

Soft soap and curtseying; with my brain, my heart and my soul. I've beaten you at your own game, my dear; at my age and with my looks, I flirted with him! And he is going to write to Oxford; at least, I am going to write to Oxford for him. Hallelujah.

MISS RONBERRY

Oxford?

MISS MOFFAT

I am entering my little pit-pony for a scholarship to Oxford, child, Oxford University!

MISS RONBERRY
(*Incredulous*)
But they don't have miners at Oxford University!

MISS MOFFAT

Well, they're going to. The lad is on this earth for eighty years at the most out of a few millions; let the proud silly ones grovel and be useful for a change, so he can step up on their backs to something better! I was bursting to say that to the Lord of the Manor, so I must vent it on you . . . Thank you for your shawl, my dear—and now you've served your purpose, you can go home—but you'd better watch out, I may beat you to the altar yet. . . . (*She shuts the front door on her, and comes back into the room, gets papers, then crosses to table—moves table, moves milk jug to sideboard and sits at table. Seated before she calls.*) Evans! (MORGAN *comes in from the study, carrying a pen, books and papers. His mantle of reserve has descended on him again; his inward rebellion is only to be guessed at from his eyes, which she does not see. He pulls the chair up to the table and sits opposite her. The daylight begins to wane*) Is this your essay on the Wealth of Nations?

MORGAN

Yes.

MISS MOFFAT

(*Reading briskly*)

Say so and underline it. Nothing irritates examiners more than that sort of vagueness. (*She hands him the exercise book*) I couldn't work this sentence out.

MORGAN

"The eighteenth century was a cauldron. Vice and elegance boiled to a simmer until the kitchen of society reeked fulminously, and the smell percolated to the marble halls above." (*Hands paper back.*)

MISS MOFFAT

D'ye know what that means?

MORGAN

Yes, Miss Moffat.

MISS MOFFAT

Because I don't. Clarify, my boy, clarify, and leave the rest to Mrs. Henry Wood. . . . "Water" with two t's . . . that's a bad lapse. . . . The Adam Smith sentence was good. Original, and clear as well. Seven out of ten, not bad, but not good —you *must* avoid long words until you know exactly what they mean. Otherwise domino. . . . Your reading?

MORGAN

Burke's "Cause of the Present Discontents."

MISS MOFFAT

Style?

MORGAN

His style appears to me . . . as if there was too much of it.

MISS MOFFAT

His style struck me as florid.

MORGAN

His style struck me as florid.

MISS MOFFAT

Again.

MORGAN

His style struck me as florid.

MISS MOFFAT

Subject matter?

MORGAN

A sound argument, falsified by—by the high color of the sentiments.

MISS MOFFAT

Mmm. "The high color of the sentiments" . . . odd but not too odd, good and stylish. . . . For next time. (*Dictating as* MORGAN *writes*) Walpole and Sheridan as representatives of their age; and no smelly cauldrons. (*Opening another book*) By the way, next Tuesday I'm starting you on Greek.

MORGAN

(*Looking up, feigning interest*)

Oh, yes?

MISS MOFFAT

(*Subduing her excitement*)

I am going to put you in for a scholarship to Oxford. (*He looks up at her, arrested.*)

MORGAN

Oxford? Where the lords go?

MISS MOFFAT

(*Amused*)

The same. I've made a simplified alphabet to begin with. It's jolly interesting after Latin. . . . (*The matter-of-factness with which she is controlling her excitement over the scholarship seems to gall him more and more; he watches her, bitterly*) Have a look at it by Tuesday, so we can make a good start. Oh, and before we go on with the lesson, I've found the nail file I mentioned. . . . (MORGAN *slams a book*) I'll show you how to use it. I had them both here somewhere. . . .

MORGAN

(*Quietly*)

I shall not need a nail file in the coal mine.

MISS MOFFAT

In the what?

MORGAN

(*Turns to her*)

I am going back to the coal mine.

MISS MOFFAT

I don't understand you. Explain yourself.

MORGAN

I do not want to learn Greek, nor to pronounce any long
English words, nor to keep my hands clean.

MISS MOFFAT
(*Staggered*)
What's the matter with you? Why not?

MORGAN

Because . . . because (*Leans over, both hands on table*) I
was born in a Welsh hayfield when my mother was helpin'
with the harvest—and I always lived in a house with no stairs,
only a ladder—and no water—and until my brothers was
killed I never sleep except three in a bed. I know that is terrible grammar but it is true.

MISS MOFFAT

What on earth has three in a bed got to do with learning
Greek?

MORGAN

It has—a lot! The last two years I have not had no proper
talk with English chaps in the mine because I was so busy
keepin' this old grammar in its place. Tryin' to better myself . . . Tryin' to better myself, the day and the night . . . !
You cannot take a nail file into the Gwesmor Arms public
bar!

MISS MOFFAT

My dear boy, file your nails at home! I never heard anything so ridiculous. Besides, you don't go to the Gwesmor
Arms!

MORGAN

Yes, I do, I have been there every afternoon for a week,
spendin' your pocket money, and I have been there now, and
that is why I can speak my mind!

MISS MOFFAT

I had no idea that you felt like this.

MORGAN

Because you are not interested in me.

MISS MOFFAT

Not interested in you?

MORGAN

(Losing control)

How can you be interested in a machine that you put a
penny in and if nothing comes out you give it a good shake?
"Evans, write me an essay; Evans, get up and bow; Evans,
what is a subjunctive!" My name is Morgan Evans, and all
my friends call me Morgan, and if there is anything gets on
the wrong side of me it is callin' me Evans! . . . And do you
know what they call me in the village? Ci bach yr ysgol! The
schoolmistress's little dog! What has it got to do with you if
my nails are dirty? Mind your own business! (*He buries his
head in his hands.*)

MISS MOFFAT

I never meant you to know this. I have spent money on you
—I don't mind that, money ought to be spent. But time is different. Your life has not yet begun, mine is half over. And
when you're a middle-aged spinster, some folk say it's pretty

115

near finished. Two years is valuable currency. I have spent two years on you. Even since that first day, the mainspring of this school has been your career. Sometimes, in the middle of the night, when I have been desperately tired, I have lain awake, making plans. Large and small. Sensible and silly. Plans, for you. And you tell me I have no interest in you. If I say any more I shall start to cry; and I haven't cried since I was younger than you are, and I'd never forgive you for that. I am going for a walk. I don't like this sort of conversation; please never mention it again. If you want to go on, be at school tomorrow. (*Going*) If not, don't.

MORGAN

I don't want your money, and I don't want your time! . . . I don't want to be thankful to no strange woman—for anything!

MISS MOFFAT

I don't understand you. I don't understand you at all. (*Taking her cloak that is hanging on door, she goes out by the front door.* MORGAN *folds his arms, takes a drink, puts bottle on the table. There is a book there. He moves book.* BESSIE *comes in from the garden. She has put her hair half up and wears earrings.*)

BESSIE

Hello! (*She clutches her leg*) Caught my knee climbin' down the rainpipe, ooh. . . . (*As he takes no notice, she crosses to kitchen door*) P'r'aps I'm invisible. . . . (*She marches into the kitchen, singing "Bell Bottom Trousers" and bangs the door behind her. Far away, the sound of singing: Men returning from the mine, harmonizing their familiar melody, "Yr Hufen Melyn."* BESSIE *returns from the kitchen*) Mum's

116

gone out. (*After a pause*) Expect she's gone to tell Mrs. Roberts about her meetin'. Though how she manages with Mrs. Roberts knowin' no English an' deaf as well . . . (*After a pause*) Talking a lot, aren't I?

MORGAN

Yes.

BESSIE

Well, I'm not deaf.

MORGAN

Been spyin'?

BESSIE

If people lock me in and take the key out of the keyhole, they can't blame me for listenin' at it. Ooh, I think she's wicked.

MORGAN

Mind your own business!

BESSIE

I won't. I like to know about everything; I like doin' all the things I like; I like sweets, I don't care if it does make me fat, and I *love* earrings. I like to shake my head like a lady. . . . (*The singing stops. A pause*) It's funny. . . . We never been by ourselves before. (*She begins to sing in Welsh. The tune is "Lliw Gwyn Rhosyn yr Haf"*) Didn't know I knew Welsh, did you? . . . You like that song, don't you? That's why I learnt it.

MORGAN

You are different when you sing.

BESSIE

Am I? . . . What's this, medicine? (*Picks up rum bottle, drinks. He takes bottle from her, takes a drink and puts it in his pocket*) Tastes like rubber. Nice, though. . . . You know —you was quite right to put her in her place. Clever chap like you learnin' lessons off a woman!

MORGAN

That's right. . . .

BESSIE
(*Soft, persuasive*)
You don't 'ave to go to Oxford! Clever chap like you!

MORGAN
(*In a whisper*)
That's right. . . . (*He turns slowly and looks at her.*)

BESSIE

What a man wants is a bit o' sympathy!

(*He looks at her, his hand on the back of the chair. It is growing faintly darker. She laughs, and begins to sing again; she turns, still singing, looks up at him, and smiles. He pushes away the chair, seizes her with violence, and kisses her passionately. Their arms entwine and the chair crashes to the floor.*)

The curtain falls

ACT TWO

Scene II

A morning in November, three months later. The room is much as it was; the potted plants have been removed; the daylight is so poor that the lamps are lit.

MRS. WATTY *is carrying in from the kitchen a small table, new and light. On it blotter, ink, pens, pencil, a duster and a cup of tea.* MISS RONBERRY *is pushing the armchair in from the study past the sofa into its old place, next to the isolated desk.*

MRS. WATTY
(*Singing*)

"I'm saved I am, I'm saved I am. . . ." (MRS. WATTY *moves the large table a bit, so as to get through, picks up small table, places it well downstage*) What would the armchair be for, miss?

MISS RONBERRY

The Squire's coming. He's invigilating. (*She opens desk drawer, and takes out package with sealed Oxford papers.*)

MRS. WATTY

What was that, please, miss?

MISS RONBERRY

The Oxford people have appointed him and Miss Moffat to watch Morgan Evans while he is sitting the scholarship, so that he cannot cheat.

MRS. WATTY

What a shame. . . . (*Still arranging furniture*) You'd never think it was nearly nine in the morning, would you?

MISS RONBERRY

It's stopped snowing.

MRS. WATTY

(*Peering out of the window*)

Only just. The milkman said the road was blocked down by the bridge.

MISS RONBERRY

How terrible if Morgan couldn't get through!

MRS. WATTY

Countin' sheep all night, I was. (*Picking up two envelopes from the floor, near the front door*) She didn't 'ave a wink neither. I could 'ear her thinkin'.

MISS RONBERRY

It is a very important day for her.

MRS. WATTY

Looks like that one's Bessie. Would you mind?

MISS RONBERRY

That means Sarah the Post got through. . . .

MRS. WATTY

She'd come the other way, down the 'ill. . . .

MISS RONBERRY

That's true . . . (*Reading*) "Dear Mum"—to think I taught her to write—"Cheltenham is terrible. Can I have a shilling? I do the steps. Madam is terrible. Your obedient girl."

MRS. WATTY

Obedient. (*Laughs*) I like that. . . . (*Throwing the letter into the wastepaper basket*) She's been away three months now, she ought to be gettin' used to it.

MISS RONBERRY

But do you not miss her?

MRS. WATTY
(*Emphatically*)
No! I don't like 'er, you know, never 'ave.

MISS RONBERRY

But, Mrs. Watty, your own daughter!

MRS. WATTY

I know, but I've never been able to take to 'er. First time I saw 'er, I said, "No." (*Going*) With 'er dad being foreign, you see.

MISS RONBERRY

But couldn't your husband have taken her abroad to his own family?

MRS. WATTY

Oh, my 'usband was quite different. British to the core. (*She goes into the kitchen.* MISS RONBERRY *blinks after her, and*

121

places writing pad on the little table. MISS MOFFAT *comes slowly downstairs. She is alert, but more subdued than the audience has yet seen her.* MISS RONBERRY *takes up the cup of tea, and watches her apprehensively.)*

MISS MOFFAT

It's stopped snowing.

MISS RONBERRY

It's a white world, as they say . . . Do you think he will get through the snow?

MISS MOFFAT

This morning he would get through anything.

MISS RONBERRY

I am so glad. I thought perhaps he—he had not been working satisfactorily. . . .

MISS MOFFAT

At ten o'clock last night I had to take his books away from him.

MISS RONBERRY

I *am* glad.

MISS MOFFAT

I hope he won't get wet—he must not (*Picks up string, plays with it*) be upset in any way. What made you think he wasn't working well?

MISS RONBERRY

Nothing, only . . . you remember the night you went for that long walk, when he might be going back to the mine?

MISS MOFFAT
(After a pause)

Yes?

MISS RONBERRY

The next morning he started studying again, and yet it seemed so different.

MISS MOFFAT

How?

MISS RONBERRY

Almost strained . . . what a silly thing to say . . . I mean, as you did not say anything more about the mine . . .

MISS MOFFAT

He didn't say any more himself. He just turned up. I didn't embrace him on both cheeks, but I said "Righto." Since which time, he has never stopped working.

MISS RONBERRY

I *am* so glad . . . Oh, this arrived from the Penlan Town Hall! It must be his birth certificate. . . .

MISS MOFFAT

Good. . . . I must send it off to the President of Trinity. Rather a nervous post-mortem from him last night; two pages to ask if the youngster's legitimate. *(Opens envelope, looks at birth certificate)* Thank Heaven he is. And no conviction for drunkenness; references have been spotless. That will help, I hope.

MISS RONBERRY

Would it not be splended if he—won!

MISS MOFFAT
(*After a pause*)
Not very likely, I am afraid. (*Moving about, nervously*)
The syllabus rather attaches importance to general knowledge
of the academic sort. His is bound to be patchy—on the exuberant side—I have had to force it; two years is not enough
even for him. If he checks himself, and does not start telling
them what they ought to think of Milton, with fair luck he
might stand a chance. He will have some pretty strong public-
school candidates against him, of course. Bound to. It depends
on how much the examiners will appreciate a highly original
intelligence.

MISS RONBERRY
(*Seated on couch*)
But wouldn't it be *exciting!*

MISS MOFFAT
Yes, it would. People run down the Universities, and always will, but it would be a wonderful thing for him. It
would be a wonderful thing for rural education all over the
country.

MISS RONBERRY
And most of all, it would be a wonderful thing for you!

MISS MOFFAT
(*Almost soliloquizing*)
I suppose so . . . It is odd to have spent so many hours with
another human being, in the closest intellectual communion—
because it has been that. I know every trick and twist of that

brain of his, exactly where it will falter and where it will gallop ahead of me—and yet not to know him at all. I woke up in the middle of the night thinking of Henry the Eighth. I have a feeling there may be a question about the old boy and the Papacy. (*Crosses to bookshelves. Takes book from shelf and makes notations on a piece of writing paper*) I'll cram one or two facts into him, the last minute . . . (*Suddenly, in a sob, with all the inward conviction of which she is capable*) Oh, God, he must win it . . . (MRS. WATTY *comes in from the kitchen, carrying a steaming cup of tea*) He must.

MRS. WATTY

(*Hands her cup of tea*)

Cup a tea! Now, ma'am, don't get in a pucker! Six more Saturday mornin's like this in the next 'alf-year, (*Gets* MISS RONBERRY's *cup from table*) remember!

MISS MOFFAT

The first paper is the important one—I expect we'll get more used to the others. . . .

MISS RONBERRY

Suppose the Squire doesn't come!

MISS MOFFAT

He will. He has got to the point of looking on the lad as a racehorse.

MISS RONBERRY

You don't think the snow might deter him?

MRS. WATTY

I just seed 'is nibs' gardener clearin' a way from the gates. Shame the red carpet gettin' so wet.

(MRS. WATTY *goes back into the kitchen.*)

MISS RONBERRY

Surely it is getting brighter this side . . . (*Looks out of the window*) Oh, I can see him! Morgan, I mean!

MISS MOFFAT

Can you?

MISS RONBERRY

Coming up the Nant, do you see? Ploughing through!

MISS MOFFAT

What is the time? (*Looks at her breast watch.*)

MISS RONBERRY

Ten minutes to!

MISS MOFFAT
(*Sitting at her desk*)

He will have just two minutes . . . (*A knock at the front door*) Good. There's the Squire . . .

MISS RONBERRY
(*Running to the door*)

He is as excited as any of us . . . (BESSIE *enters the room, followed by* MR. JONES) Bessie . . . But it cannot be you, your mother has just received . . .

BESSIE

I left the same day I posted it. (*She is shabbily dressed, in semi-grown-up fashion, and wears a cloak. Her manner is staccato, nervy and defiant.* MR. JONES *closes door, leaves* BESSIE's *bag near desk. She faces* MISS MOFFAT, *who stares at her, puzzled.*)

MISS MOFFAT

This is unexpected.

BESSIE

Isn't it just? I have been travellin' all night, quite a wreck. I woke Mr. Jones up and he got the stationmaster to drive us over in his trap, in the snow—nice, wasn't it? (*She is trying not to be frightened, and not succeeding. The conversation from now on quickens and grows more nervous.*)

MISS MOFFAT

You have arrived at an inconvenient time.

(MISS RONBERRY *crosses Left above table.*)

BESSIE

Fancy.

MISS MOFFAT

Have you come to see your mother?

BESSIE

No. (*She plucks up courage and sits suddenly in the arm-chair.* MISS MOFFAT *frowns and rises.*)

MISS MOFFAT

Then why are you here?

127

BESSIE

Questions and answers, just like school again!

MISS MOFFAT

Why have you brought this girl here this morning?

MR. JONES

I did not bring her, Miss Moffat, she brought me. . . .

MISS MOFFAT

Whom have you come to see?

BESSIE

You.

MISS MOFFAT

Me? (BESSIE *does not speak*) I can give you exactly one minute of my time. (*Pause*) Is it money? (*As* BESSIE *does not answer, impatiently to the others*) Will you wait in the study? (MR. JONES *follows* MISS RONBERRY *into the study*) One minute. . . . Quickly!

BESSIE

Why?

MISS MOFFAT

Morgan Evans is sitting for his Oxford examination here this morning.

BESSIE

Well, 'e needn't.

MISS MOFFAT

What do you mean?

BESSIE

Because he won't ever be goin' to Oxford.

MISS MOFFAT

Why not?

BESSIE

Because there's goin' to be a little stranger. (*A pause*) I'm going to have a little stranger. (*She begins to whimper into her handkerchief, half acting, half nerves and excitement.* MISS MOFFAT *stares at her.*)

MISS MOFFAT

You're lying.

BESSIE

Doctor Brett, The Firs, Cheltenham . . . And if you don't believe it's Morgan Evans, you ask 'im about that night you locked me up—the night you had the words with him!

MISS MOFFAT

I see . . . (*With a sudden cry*) Why couldn't I have seen before! (*Her eyes rest on the examination table. She collects herself, desperately*) Does he know?

BESSIE

I've come to tell 'im! I was ever so upset, of course, and now I've lost me place. Oh, she was artful. He'll have to marry me, or I'll show him up, 'cause I must give the little stranger a name. . . .

129

MISS MOFFAT

(*Exasperated beyond endurance*)

Stop saying "little stranger"! If you must have a baby, then call it a baby! . . . Have you told anybody?

BESSIE

Mr. Jones, that's all. . . .

MISS RONBERRY

(*Peering timidly through the study door*)

The Squire is coming up the road! (*She goes back into the study.*)

BESSIE

I'll wait here for him.

MISS MOFFAT

For the next three hours, he must not be disturbed. You are not going to see him . . .

BESSIE

You can't bully me, the way I am! (*Rising, and facing her across the examination table, the resentment of two years pouring out, real hysteria this time*) 'Asn't sunk in yet, 'as it? I'm teaching *you* something, am I? You didn't know things like that went on, did you? Why? You couldn't see what was goin' on under your nose, 'cause you're too busy managin' everythin'! Well, you can't manage him any longer, 'cause he's got to manage me now, the way I am, he's got to—

(MR. JONES *pokes his head round the study door; he is in a state of panic.* MISS RONBERRY *hovers behind him.*)

MR. JONES

Morgan Evans has turned the corner up the hill . . .

MISS RONBERRY

So there isn't much time!

(MR. JONES *follows* MISS RONBERRY *back into the study.*)

MISS MOFFAT

I'm afraid I am going to do a little managing now. You are going into the kitchen, where your mother will make you breakfast; you will then lie down, and as soon as this session is finished we will go upstairs and talk it all over when we are a little calmer.

(*A knock at the front door.*)

BESSIE

He's here! I got to see him! (BESSIE *starts up.* MISS MOFFAT *detains her.*)

MISS MOFFAT

If you try and disobey me, I shall not answer for the consequences. (*Holds her wrist.*)

BESSIE

(*Cowed*)

You wouldn't dare lay a finger on me . . .

MISS MOFFAT

Oh, yes, I would. If you attempt to stay in this room, or to blab to anybody about this before we have had that talk—even your mother . . . I am in a pretty nervous state myself, this morning, and I shall strike you so hard that I shall probably kill you. . . . I mean every word of that.

(*Another knock, more impatient. She quells* BESSIE *with her look; crosses and holds open the kitchen door.*)

BESSIE

(*Laughs*)

I don't mind. Three hours'll go soon enough. (*She goes into the kitchen.* MISS MOFFAT *shuts the door after her, straightens herself, and opens the front door. The* SQUIRE *enters, in Inverness cape and hat, stamping the snow from his boots; he carries several periodicals, chiefly sporting and dramatic. The rest of the scene is played very quickly.*)

MISS MOFFAT

(*Takes his coat and hat*)

So very sorry—how kind of you—such a dreadful day . . . (*Hangs* SQUIRE's *coat on door.*)

THE SQUIRE

Not at all, Mistress Pedagogue, anything for a lark. . . . Glad it isn't me, what . . . ? I've got a spiffy bit of news for you.

MISS MOFFAT

Yes?

THE SQUIRE

I've bought the barn from Sir Herbert, and we can move the whole shoot next door by March. What d'ye think?

MISS MOFFAT

Wonderful . . .

THE SQUIRE

We can knock a door straight through here to the barn— aren't ye pleased about it?

MISS MOFFAT

(*Going to the desk, hardly aware of what she is doing, as* MISS RONBERRY *runs in from the study*)

Yes, but you know, this examination, (*Knock at front door*) rather worrying . . .

MISS RONBERRY

Good morning, Squire! Terrible weather . . .

THE SQUIRE

Beastly—

(MISS RONBERRY *opens the front door and lets* MORGAN *in. She closes the door before she takes his overcoat, cap and muffler. He has been hurrying, but he is quiet and calm.*)

MISS MOFFAT

Wet?

MORGAN

No, thank you. Good day, sir . . .

133

MISS RONBERRY

Let me take your things . . .

MORGAN

Thank you . . .

MISS MOFFAT

Before I open the papers, I have a feeling they may bring up Henry the Eighth. Memorize these two facts, will you? (*Hands him a paper.*)

MISS RONBERRY

(*Puts down a sprig of white heather*)

White heather—just a thought! (*She runs into the study.*)

MORGAN

Thank you . . .

THE SQUIRE

Good luck, my boy.

MORGAN

Thank you, sir . . .

THE SQUIRE

Glad it isn't me!

(MORGAN *hands her the paper.*)

MR. JONES

(*Pops his head round the study door*)

Pob llwyddiant, ymachgeni!

MORGAN

Diolch—

134

(MISS MOFFAT *throws paper in the basket.* MR. JONES
goes back into the study. MORGAN *sits at the table.*)

MISS MOFFAT

Name and particulars, to save time. And don't get exuberant.

MORGAN

No.

MISS MOFFAT

Or illegible.

MORGAN

No.

(*Pause.*)

THE SQUIRE

But aren't *you* going to wish my little protégé good
fortune?

MISS MOFFAT
(*After a pause, to* MORGAN)

Good luck.

MORGAN

Thank you.

(*The clock begins to strike nine.*)

MISS MOFFAT

Ready? (MORGAN *nods. She cuts the envelope and places
the examination paper in front of him. She looks at the
duplicate paper of questions, smiles*) Henry the Eighth!

135

(*She sits in the armchair. The* SQUIRE *embarks on his periodical.* MORGAN *begins to write.* MISS MOFFAT *raises her head, looks anxiously toward the kitchen, then steadfastly at* MORGAN, *her lip trembling. A pause. The only sound is the scratch of a pen.*)

The curtain falls slowly

ACT THREE

ACT THREE

SCENE: *An afternoon in July. Seven months later.*

The school has been moved next door, and the room is much less crowded; the small table is back in the window recess, the armchair is in its old position; the large table, however, is no longer behind the sofa with its chair, its place being taken by three small school desks facing the front door; between the front door and the bay window a blackboard on its easel faces the audience at an angle, with "Elizabeth, known as Good Q. Bess" written on it in block letters.

MR. JONES *stands in command beside the blackboard. In two of the school desks sit* IDWAL *and* ROBBART, *each poring over his slate. On the settle sit the* SQUIRE, *downstage, his arms folded like a pupil, his eyes fixed on* MR. JONES, *and next to him* OLD TOM, *upstage, laboriously copying the inscription on to his slate.* MR. JONES *crosses to* IDWAL'S *desk, then to* ROBBART'S *desk; looks at their work.*

OLD TOM
(*Muttering, as he writes*)
Elissabeth—known—as—what in goodness is a "k" doin' there, that iss a pussell for me . . .

MR. JONES
"I wandered lonely as a cloud." From "The Daffodils," by Wordsworth.

139

(*The boys scratch busily. The* squire *begins to nod sleepily.* miss ronberry *hurries in from the garden.*)

miss ronberry

What is the capital of Sweden?

mr. jones

Stockholm.

miss ronberry

Thank you. (*She hurries back into the garden.*)

old tom

Please, sir, how many l's in "daffodils"?

the squire

Damned if I know.

(john owen *comes in by the study door.*)

john

Please, Mistar Jones, Form Two Arithmetic Report—Miss Moffat says will you come in school with it. (*He goes back.* mr. jones *follows him through the study after getting book and papers from the sideboard. The* squire *snores.*)

robbart

Mae o'n cysgu. Tyd. Idwal . . .

old tom

Plenty Welsh at home, not in the class, please, by request, scoundrels and notty boys!

IDWAL
(*Rises*)

Squire iss 'avin' a snore. Nai ddangos rwbeth ichi— (*He rises, runs to the blackboard, takes the chalk and the duster, and swiftly rubs out and adds to the inscription till it reads: "NO . . . GOOD . . . BESSIE." The* SQUIRE *grunts. As he strikes the period the* SQUIRE *sticks his foot out. He says "Na-fe."*)

MR. JONES
(*Returning*)

Now history. (*Stumbles over the* SQUIRE'S *foot. Crosses to blackboard*) Excuse me . . . Elizabeth . . . (*He sees the inscription and stops short. He turns on the others, grave and perturbed*) Who did this?

IDWAL

Please, Mr. Jones, perhaps it iss some terrible dunce that want to know what iss Bessie Watty been doin' the last few months.

(*A pause.*)

MR. JONES

Whoever it was . . . (SQUIRE *rises*) I am going to cane him! It was not you, sir, by any chance?

THE SQUIRE

Not guilty. . . . Bessie Watty? Little Cockney thing? Nice ankles?

141

MR. JONES

I do not know, sir . . . (*Boys snicker*) Silence, boys! Where is my duster?

(SQUIRE *goes to window and looks out.*)

THE SQUIRE

Still no sign of him.

MR. JONES

You mean Morgan Evans, sir? (*Boys look up*) He is not expected before the train leaving Oxford half-past one . . .

THE SQUIRE

There's a sporting chance the Viva finished yesterday, and I sent the wagonette to meet the one-ten.

MR. JONES

Do you think that he may know the result when he arrives?

THE SQUIRE

I doubt it. Miss Moffat said we'll hear by letter in a day or two. . . . (*Rising restlessly and going toward the front door*) Think I'll propel the old pins down the highway, just in case . . .

IDWAL

Please, sir, what sort of a place is Oxford?

THE SQUIRE

Dunno, I'm sure. Cambridge myself. (*He goes. Leaves door open.*)

MR. JONES

(*At blackboard*)

Now history. Repeat after me . . .

IDWAL

Please, Mr. Jones, tell us about Bessie Watty?

MR. JONES

If you are kept in tomorrow, I will give you religion. Repeat after me . . . (*The school bell rings*) Dismiss! (ROBBART *rises and straps books.* MR. JONES *goes to desk and tidies papers.* SARAH *hurries in from the front door. She is dressed in her best, in the traditional Welsh peasant costume with a steeple hat.*)

SARAH

Please, sir, have you got my father— (*Seeing* OLD TOM) tiddona, 'nhad, ma'dy frwas di'n oeri . . .

OLD TOM

English, daughter, in the class, pliss!

SARAH

You are an old soft, your porridge it iss gettin' cold and you have not got your sleep . . .

OLD TOM

But I got my Queen Elizabeth . . .

(SARAH *takes his slate, puts it on* ROBBART'S *desk.*)

SARAH

And in the mornin' you got your rheumatics—come on!
(SARAH *helps* OLD TOM *to rise.* MISS RONBERRY *comes in from
the garden.*)

ROBBART

Sarah Pugh, what you all clobbered up for?

SARAH

Because for Morgan Evans.

MR. JONES

Is there some news?

MISS RONBERRY

About Morgan? Oh, quickly!

SARAH

Not yet, Mistar Jones. But when it comes, I know it iss
good news, so what do I do? I open the dresser, out the
lavender bags and into my Sundays! Home (*Starts to door
with* OLD TOM), dada, for Sundays . . .

MR. JONES

Before we have definite news, that is unwise . . .

SARAH

John Goronwy Jones, pliss, sir, you are an old soft. Everybody is ready to meet him by the Nant! The grocer got his
fiddle . . .

IDWAL

And William Williams the public got his cornet!

ROBBART

And with me on me mouth organ . . . (*Strikes chord on mouth organ.*)

SARAH

And me singin'!

ROBBART

Tyd, Idwal— (*He runs out by the front door, followed by* IDWAL.)

MISS RONBERRY

Perhaps preparing for news to be good means that it will be.

MR. JONES

Everything is preordained. Morgan Evans has either won the scholarship, or lost it.

MISS RONBERRY

Let us all say together, "Morgan Evans has won the scholarship!"

ALL
(*Except* MR. JONES)

"Morgan Evans has won the scholarship!"

SARAH
(*To* OLD TOM)

Tiddana, 'nhad—

OLD TOM

I never got a letter yet, and nobody never put Sundays on for me. . . . (*He goes out by the front door.* SARAH *starts to go.* MISS RONBERRY'S *eye catches the blackboard.*)

145

MISS RONBERRY

"No . . . (SARAH *comes back*) good . . . Bessie." Good gracious!

MR. JONES

Where *is* my duster? (*Looks behind blackboard.*)

MISS RONBERRY

What does that mean?

SARAH

Bessie Watty. Miss Ronberry, where is she?

(MR. JONES *finds duster at* IDWAL'S *desk*)

MISS RONBERRY

I don't know, dear.

SARAH

Miss Moffat she hears from her, in my post office. (JONES *erases blackboard*) We wass all wonderin'. (*She goes out by the front door.*)

MISS RONBERRY

Well, I have been wondering too! She came back that morning and just went away again. Morgan Evans was telling me only the day he left for Oxford that he didn't even *see* her. Where is she?

MR. JONES

It is more important to know if Morgan Evans has won or not.

MISS RONBERRY

I know . . . If he hasn't, it will break her heart.

MR. JONES

Would she feel it so keen as all that?

MISS RONBERRY

I used not to think so, but since that day they have been so much better friends, it has been a pleasure to hear them conversing. Perhaps it is the strain of all these examinations . . .

(MISS MOFFAT *comes in from the study with exercise book, chuckling.*)

MISS MOFFAT

Gwyneth Thomas, the plasterer's eldest, essay on Knowledge. "Be good, sweet maid, and let who will be clever"—I wonder if the Reverend Kingsley had any idea what a smack in the eye that was for lady teachers? And then Gwyneth Thomas starts (*Reading*): "It is not nice to know too much, I wish to be like Miss Ronberry, Miss Moffat is different, she knows everything." Any news?

MR. JONES

Not yet.

MISS MOFFAT

I thought not. . . . (*A pause*) Where is the Squire?

MR. JONES

Gone to see if there is any sign.

MISS MOFFAT

Thank the Lord. That man is really becoming a nuisance. He gave up Henley to be here this week. Did you know?

MR. JONES

You do not appear nervous?

MISS MOFFAT

I am past being nervous. If he has won, I shan't believe it. Flatly.

MISS RONBERRY

And if he has lost?

MISS MOFFAT

If he has lost . . . (*After a pause*) We must proceed as if nothing had happened. The sun rises and sets every day, and while it does we have jolly well got to revolve round it; the time to sit up and take notice will be the day it decides not to appear. In the meantime, Mr. Jones, your report is on your desk. Miss Ronberry, Form Two are waiting for your music like a jungle of hungry parakeets.

MISS RONBERRY

Yes, Miss Moffat.

> (*They retire meekly through the study.* MISS MOFFAT *is alone. She looks at her watch; her armor loosens perceptibly; she is on edge and apprehensive. She goes toward the stairs, but before she reaches them the garden door opens suddenly and* MORGAN *appears. He wears a new dark suit, carries a travelling bag and his cap, and looks dusty and tired. His manner is excited and unstable; he is alternately eager and intensely depressed. She stares at him, not daring to speak.*)

MORGAN

I caught the early train. I knew they would all be watching for me, so I got out at Llanmorfedd and got a lift to Gwaenygam.

MISS MOFFAT

Does that mean . . . ?

MORGAN

Oh, no news. Except that I am not hopeful.

MISS MOFFAT

Why not?

MORGAN

They talked to me for one hour at the Viva . . .

MISS MOFFAT

That doesn't mean anything. Go on.

MORGAN

They jumped down hard on the New Testament question. As you said they would. . . . You are very pale.

MISS MOFFAT

Better than a raging fever. Go on.

MORGAN

I spent five minutes explaining why Saint Paul sailed from a town three hundred miles inland.

MISS MOFFAT

Oh, dear. (*Their manner together has changed since we*

149

last saw them together. They are hardly at all teacher and pupil, superior and inferior, adult and child. They are more like two friends held solidly by a bond unsentimental and un-self-conscious. MORGAN'S *English has immensely improved, and he expresses himself with ease.*) Parnell?

MORGAN

Parnell . . . (*Smiles*) Oh, yes . . . I was going to stick up for the old chap, but when they started off with "that fellow Parnell," I told the tale against him for half an hour. I wasn't born a Welshman for nothing.

MISS MOFFAT

Ha . . . And the French?

MORGAN

Not good. I said "naturellement" to everything, but it didn't fit every time.

MISS MOFFAT

And the Greek verbs?

MORGAN

They were sarcastic.

MISS MOFFAT

Did the President send for you?

MORGAN

I had half an hour with him . . .

MISS MOFFAT

You did?

MORGAN

Yes, but so did the other nine candidates! He was a very kind and grand old gentleman sitting in a drawing room the size of Penlan Town Hall. I talked about religion, the same as you said . . .

MISS MOFFAT

(*Correcting him, mechanically*)

Just as you advised . . .

MORGAN

Just as you advised. He asked me if I had ever had strong drink, and I looked him straight in the eye and said "No."

MISS MOFFAT

Oh!

MORGAN

I was terrible—terribly nervous. My collar stud flew off, and I had to hold on to my collar with one hand, and he did not seem impressed with me at all. . . . He was very curious about you. (*Rises*) Did you know there was an article in the *Morning Post* about the school?

MISS MOFFAT

Was there? . . . But what else makes you despondent?

MORGAN

The other candidates. They appeared to me brilliant. I had never thought they would be, somehow! Two from Eton and one from Harrow—one of them very rich. I had never thought a scholarship man might be rich. He had his own servant.

MISS MOFFAT

Gosh!

MORGAN

And the servant looked so like my father I thought it was at first. . . . And, as I was leaving, the examiners appeared to be sorry for me in some way, and I received the impression that I had failed. I . . .

MISS MOFFAT

When shall we know?

MORGAN

The day after tomorrow. They are writing to you.

MISS MOFFAT

The villagers are all in their best, and talking about a holiday tomorrow. It is very stupid of them, because if you have failed it will make you still more sick at heart . . .

MORGAN

If I have failed? (*In sudden desperation*) Don't speak about it!

MISS MOFFAT

But we must! You faced the idea the day you left for Oxford . . .

MORGAN

I know, but I have *been* to Oxford, and come back, since then! I have come back—from the world! Since the day I was born, I have been a prisoner behind a stone wall, and now somebody has given me a leg-up to have a look at the other side. . . . They cannot drag me back again, they cannot. They *must* give me a push and send me over!

MISS MOFFAT

I've never heard you talk so much since I've known you.

MORGAN

That is just it! I *can* talk, now! The three days I have been there, I have been talking my head off!

MISS MOFFAT

Ha! If three days at Oxford can do that to you, what would you be like at the end of three years?

MORGAN

That's just it again. It would be everything I need, everything! Starling and I spent three hours one night discussin' the law—Starling, you know, the brilliant one. . . . The words came pouring out of me—all the words that I had learnt and written down and never spoken. I suppose I was talking nonsense, but I was at least holding a conversation! I suddenly realized that I had never done it before—I had never been *able* to do it. (*With a strong Welsh accent*) "How are you, Morgan? Nice day, Mr. Jones! Not bad for the harvest." A vocabulary of twenty words; all the thoughts that you have given to me were being stored away as if they were always going to be useless—locked up and rotting away —a lot of questions with nobody to answer them, a lot of statements with nobody to contradict them. . . . And there I was with Starling, nineteen to the dozen. I came out of his

153

rooms that night, and I walked down the High. That's their High Street, you know.

MISS MOFFAT

(*Nodding, drinking in the torrent with the most intense pleasure*)

Yes, yes. . . .

MORGAN

I looked up, and there was a moon behind Magd—Maudlin. Not the same moon I have seen over the Nant, a different face altogether. Everybody seemed to be walking very fast, with their gowns on, in the moonlight. The bells were ringing, and I was walking faster than anybody and I felt—well, the same as on the rum in the old days!

MISS MOFFAT

Go on.

MORGAN

All of a sudden, with one big rush, against that moon, and against that High Street—I saw this room; you and me sitting here studying, and all those books—and everything I have ever learnt from those books, and from you, was lighted up—like a magic lantern: Ancient Rome, Greece, Shakespeare, Carlyle, Milton. . . . Everything had a meaning, because I was in a new world—my world! And so it came to me why you worked like a slave to make me ready for this scholarship. (*Lamely*) I've finished.

MISS MOFFAT

I didn't want you to stop.

154

MORGAN

I had not been drinking.

MISS MOFFAT

I know.

MORGAN

I can talk to you too, now.

MISS MOFFAT

Yes. I'm glad.

(*The* SQUIRE *comes in from the front door.* MORGAN *rises.*)

THE SQUIRE

No sign of the feller-me-lad, dang it . . . (*Hangs hat on door*) Evans! (*Goes to* MORGAN, *shakes hands*) There you are!

MORGAN

Good day, sir.

THE SQUIRE

Well?

MORGAN

They are sending the result through the post.

THE SQUIRE

The devil they are. (*To* MISS MOFFAT, *as he sits in armchair*) D'ye know I am finding this waiting a definite strain?

(MR. JONES *runs in from the study, stops at foot of stairs.*)

155

MR. JONES

Somebody said they had seen Morgan . . .

MORGAN

Day after tomorrow.

MR. JONES

Oh. . . .

THE SQUIRE

Examiners all right, my boy?

MORGAN

Rather sticky, sir.

THE SQUIRE

Lot of old fogies, I expect. Miss Moffat, I told you you ought to have made inquiries at the other place. However . . .

(MISS RONBERRY *runs in from the study.*)

MISS RONBERRY

Somebody said they had seen . . .

THE SQUIRE AND MR. JONES

The day after tomorrow!

MISS RONBERRY

Oh . . . How are you, Morgan, dear . . . ?

MR. JONES

(*Wandering out to the porch*)

The suspense is terrible.

156

THE SQUIRE

I know.

MR. JONES

Even the little children are worrying about— (*He stops short; he has seen somebody coming down the village street; he looks again, doubtfully; starts, then peers anxiously into the room. Everybody is preoccupied. He comes into the room, shuts the door, and stands a moment with his back to it*) Morgan, my boy, are you not exhausted after your journey? Would you not like something to eat?

MORGAN

I am rather hungry, yes . . .

MISS MOFFAT

But how stupid of me! Watty will boil you an egg . . . Come along . . .

MORGAN
(*Rising*)
Thank you. Excuse me . . . (*He follows* MISS MOFFAT *out.*)

MISS MOFFAT
(*As she goes into the kitchen*)
Did they spot the Dryden howler?

MORGAN

No.

(MR. JONES *goes to the kitchen door and closes it after them.*)

157

THE SQUIRE

You seemed very anxious to get 'em out of the room. What's the matter . . . ?

(*The front door opens and* BESSIE *walks in. She has completely changed; she might be ten years older. Her hair is up; she wears a cheaply smart costume, with a cape, and looks dazzlingly pretty in a loose opulent style. Her whole personality has blossomed. A pause. They stare at her.*)

BESSIE

Hallo!

THE SQUIRE

How d'ye do . . . ?

BESSIE

I'm very well indeed, thanks, and how are you, blooming? (*Her accent is nearer the ladylike than it has been yet.*)

THE SQUIRE

Yes, thanks . . . What *is* this?

MISS RONBERRY

I really couldn't say . . . Good gracious, it's Bessie W—

BESSIE

Right first time. Hello, Miss Ronberry, how's geography, the world still goin' round in circles? Hello, Mr. Jones, flirty as ever?

158

THE SQUIRE

And to what do we owe this honor?

BESSIE

Well, it's like this . . .

MR. JONES
(*Desperately*)
Miss Ronberry, will you please return to your class . . . ?

MISS RONBERRY

They are quite safe. I left Mary Davies in charge . . .

BESSIE

No, you don't. We've had too many secrets as it is.

MR. JONES

Three days ago she sent money to you. Did you not receive the letter?

BESSIE

Yes, I did, and all the others, till I was sick of 'em.

THE SQUIRE

What *is* all this?

BESSIE

Last week I was glancing through the *Mid-Wales Gazette*, and I'm here to congratulate a certain young gent in case he has won that scholarship.

MR. JONES

Oh!

MISS RONBERRY

But what has that got to do with you?

BESSIE

You see, Miss, it's like this . . .

MR. JONES
(*In a last effort to stop her*)
Don't say it—don't say it!

BESSIE

Four weeks yesterday, I had a baby.

(*A pause.* MISS RONBERRY *and* THE SQUIRE *stare at her.*
MR. JONES *gives a sigh of impotent despair.*)

THE SQUIRE

You had a what?

BESSIE

A baby. Seven pounds thirteen ounces.

THE SQUIRE

Good God, how ghastly.

MR. JONES
(*Turns to her*)
It is a disgustin' subject and . . .

BESSIE

It isn't disgusting at all. If I had a wedding ring you'd
think it was sweet.

THE CORN IS GREEN

(MRS. WATTY *hurries in from the kitchen.*)

MRS. WATTY

Morgan Evans's luggage. Excuse me, sir. (*Catches sight of the* SQUIRE's *serious face*) Oh! . . . (*Fearfully*) Any news?

THE SQUIRE

Well, yes. . . .

MRS. WATTY

Bessie! (*Drops the bag in her excitement*) My, you do look a dollymop! Excuse me, sir . . .

THE SQUIRE

Say anything you like . . .

MRS. WATTY

Where d'you get them bracelets?

BESSIE

Present.

MRS. WATTY

Oh, that's all right. Where 'ave you been, you madam?

BESSIE

Turnin' you into a granny.

MRS. WATTY

A gra— (*Both laugh*) Well, *fancy!*

(MISS MOFFAT *comes in from the kitchen.*)

MISS MOFFAT

And I should try and have a sleep if I were you . . .

MRS. WATTY

You could 'ave knocked me down with a feather!

BESSIE

Hello. (MISS MOFFAT *stops short*) I've just been telling them you-know-what. (*It is plain she is no longer afraid of* MISS MOFFAT. *The latter looks from one to the other, helplessly.*)

THE SQUIRE

And now I think it's time you told us who the fellow is. I am going to take drastic proceedings . . .

MRS. WATTY

That's right, dear. Who is it?

BESSIE

Well, as a matter of fact . . .

MISS MOFFAT
(*With a cry*)

No! I'll pay you anything . . . Anything!

BESSIE

It's no good, miss. (MISS MOFFAT *turns away*) It's Morgan Evans.

(*A pause.*)

THE SQUIRE

What!

MISS RONBERRY
(*Dazed*)

I don't believe it . . .

MRS. WATTY
(*Really upset, to* MISS MOFFAT)

Oh, ma'am.

MISS MOFFAT

I've been dreading this, for months. In a terrible way it's a relief.

BESSIE

Bamboozlin' me every week he was in the gutter!

MISS MOFFAT

Lies, all lies, and I was glad to be telling them . . .

MISS RONBERRY
(*Suddenly articulate*)

I can't go on listening! I can't bear it! It all comes of meddling with this teaching. She was in my class . . . What *would* Papa have said! This horrible unnatural happening . . .

MISS MOFFAT
(*Exasperated beyond endurance*)

Don't talk nonsense! It isn't horrible, and it isn't unnatural! On the contrary, it's nature giving civilization a nasty tweak of the nose. The schoolmistress *has* learnt a lesson, but it's a little late now.

BESSIE
(*Rising*)

Where is he?

MRS. WATTY

Over my dead body, my girl . . .

BESSIE

She's right, mum, it's too late. I got a four-weeks-old baby, kickin', healthy and hungry, and I haven't got a husband to keep him, so his father's got to turn *into* my husband. That's only fair, isn't it?

THE SQUIRE
(*Rises*)

I'm sorry, Miss Moffat, but I'm inclined to agree . . .

BESSIE

I'll call him . . .

MR. JONES

There is no need to call him!

THE SQUIRE

What's the matter with you?

MR. JONES

I am sorry to say that I have a strong feeling of affection for this young woman.

BESSIE
(*Sitting again on the sofa, amused*)

Oh, yes—I've got the face of an angel, haven't I?

MR. JONES

And I am willing to do my duty by rehabilitating her in wedlock, and bestowing on the infant every advantage by bringing it up a Baptist.

THE SQUIRE

Are you serious?

MR. JONES

I am always serious.

BESSIE
(*To* MISS MOFFAT)
You'd like that, wouldn't you?

MRS. WATTY

Now we're not pretendin' it's a windfall, but for a girl who's took the wrong turnin' it's a present! And you'd 'ave your own way in everything—wouldn't she, sir?

MR. JONES
(*Eagerly*)

Of course . . .

MRS. WATTY

Well, will you?

BESSIE

No. I won't. I'd like to oblige . . . (*Laughs*) but, really, I couldn't! (MR. JONES *turns away*) Besides, my friend would be furious.

MRS. WATTY
(*Clutching at straws*)

Your friend?

BESSIE

Ever such a nice gentleman, sporting, quite a swell, owns a race-course. (MRS. WATTY *looks suspicious*) You needn't look like that. I only met him ten weeks ago. I'd started servin' behind a bar for fun. I was the picture of health and ever so lucky in the counter bein' very high.

THE SQUIRE

I have never heard such a conversation outside a police court. I am seeking the safety of my own quarters. Anything I can do, Miss Moffat . . .

BESSIE

I suppose *you* wouldn't care to stake a claim?

THE SQUIRE

Good gracious . . .

(*Exits.* BESSIE *laughs.*)

MISS MOFFAT

Doesn't this man of yours want to marry you?

BESSIE

'E won't talk of anything else, but he won't have the baby. He says it would be different if the father'd been a pal of his—you can understand it, really, can't you? So I've got to give up my friend and marry Morgan Evans. Pity, 'cos my friend worships me. Ever since I left he keeps on sending me telegrams. I just got two at the station, and I expect I'll get some more tonight, isn't it rich? (*Laughs*) Mr. Jones wouldn't consider the baby without me?

MISS RONBERRY

The baby without you! Your child! What about your— your mother love?

BESSIE

I expect you'll think I'm a wicked girl, but d'you know, I haven't got any!

MISS RONBERRY

Oh, what a vile thing to say, vile . . .

BESSIE

(*Rising*)

Now listen, dear. . . . You're seeing this baby as if it was yours, aren't you—you'd think the world of it, wouldn't you?

MISS RONBERRY

It would mean everything to me— (*Turns away*) my whole life. . . .

BESSIE

I have a pretty near idea how old you are. When I'm your age I'll love the idea of a baby, but life hasn't begun yet for me. I'm just getting a taste for it. What do *I* want with a baby?

MRS. WATTY

That's what we all waht to know!

BESSIE

Yes, mum, but you know what it is . . .

167

MISS RONBERRY

You're inhuman, that's what you are! To think you don't want it. . . . (*She is on the point of bursting into foolish tears, and runs into study.*)

BESSIE

I didn't mean to be nasty—but inhuman indeed! I didn't want the baby, nobody would have, but I was careful so it'd be all right, and now it is all right I want it to have a good time. But *I* want a good time too! I *could* have left it on a doorstep, couldn't I? But I must see it's in good hands—and that's why I've come to Morgan Evans.

MISS MOFFAT

You want to make him marry you, on the chance he will become fond enough of the child to ensure its future—your conscience will be clear and later you can go off on your own?

BESSIE

I shouldn't be surprised . . .

MISS MOFFAT

In the meantime, it's worth while to ruin a boy on—on the threshold of . . .

BESSIE

I don't know anything about that, I'm sure. (*Calling*) Morgan!

MISS MOFFAT

(*Intercepting her, desperately*)

Ssh! Wait a minute, wait. . . . There may be a way out—there must be . . .

MRS. WATTY

Gawd bless us, ma'am—I got it!

MISS MOFFAT

What?

MRS. WATTY

Why can't you adopt it? (BESSIE *and* MR. JONES *stare from her to* MISS MOFFAT.)

MISS MOFFAT

Don't be ridiculous.

MRS. WATTY

Would that do you, Bessie?

BESSIE

Well! I never thought . . .

MRS. WATTY

Would it, though?

BESSIE

(*After consideration*)

Yes, it would.

MISS MOFFAT

It *would?* . . . But . . . But what would *I* do with a baby? I—I don't even know what they look like!

MRS. WATTY

They're lovely little things. Now it's all arranged . . .

MISS MOFFAT

But it would be fantastic . . .

BESSIE

(*Going up to her, eagerly*)

Oh, do, please, it'd put *everything* to rights! I would know
the baby was safe. Morgan Evans need never know a thing
about it. I can marry my friend, and it will all be beautiful!
He might grow like his father and turn out quite nice, and
anyway I'm not really so bad, you know. And he's on the
bottle now—and I could give all the instructions before I go.
And you could have it straight away, see, because if it's going
I don't want to have it with me longer than I can help, see,
because I'd only start gettin' fond of it, see . . .

MRS. WATTY

Come on, ma'am, you've been pushin' us about for three
years, now we'll give *you* a shove!

MISS MOFFAT

But it's mad—I tell you . . .

MRS. WATTY

Not as mad as takin' *me* in was, with my trouble! You've
allus been like that, you might as well go on . . .

MISS MOFFAT

But I was never meant to be a mother. I'm not like Miss
Ronberry. Why, *she* is the one to do it . . .

MR. JONES

(*Hastily*)

She would never agree. We were discussin' Marged Hopkins going to the workhouse—and she said she could never hold with any child born like that.

MISS MOFFAT

Oh . . . I suppose it would worry some folk. . . . But, Watty, you're the grandmother, and surely you . . .

MRS. WATTY

Oh, I couldn't! I don't bear it no ill-will, but every penny I get goes to the Corpse. You're the one, dear, really you are.

MISS MOFFAT

Bessie Watty, do you mean that if I do not adopt this child, you . . .

BESSIE

I will have to tell Morgan Evans, and he will have to marry me, I swear that.

MISS MOFFAT

And do you swear that you would never let Morgan Evans know the truth?

BESSIE

I swear. If there are any questions, I'll say it was my friend's.

(*A pause.*)

MISS MOFFAT

Then—I give in.

BESSIE

That's lovely. My friend *will* be pleased. I'll pop back to the public-house for his telegram and send him a nice one back. Good-bye, all, we'll arrange details later, shall we? My friend gave me this buckle, isn't it nice? He offered me a tiny one, real, but I think the false is prettier, don't you?

MR. JONES
(*As she turns to go*)
Are you going to take up a life of sin?

BESSIE
(*Smiling*)
I shouldn't be surprised. I'm only really meself with a lot of gentlemen round me, y'know, and a nice glass o' port will never come amiss, neither. (*To* MRS. WATTY) That cold water didn't really do the trick, mum, did it? . . . (*To* MISS MOF-FAT, *serious for a moment*) Good-bye . . . I only did it to spite you, y'know.

MR. JONES
You are not fit to touch the hem of her garment.

BESSIE
Oh, yes, I am! Just because she's read a lot o' books. Books, books! Look at 'em all! I got more out of life at my age than she has out o' them all her days—and I'll get a lot more yet! What d'you bet me? (*She goes out by the front door, leaves door open.* MRS. WATTY *closes the door after her.*)

MRS. WATTY
That's settled . . . (*Comes down.*)

(*The voices of children, in the barn, singing "Dacw'n-ghariad."*)

172

MR. JONES
(*Making for the study door*)
For which we must be truly thankful . . .

(MORGAN *walks in quickly from the kitchen. He goes straight to* MISS MOFFAT; *his face is white and shocked. They stare at him, instinctively silent.*)

MORGAN

Has she gone?

MISS MOFFAT

Why?

MORGAN

The Squire just came in to see me.

MISS MOFFAT

The fool! The idiotic fool . . .

MORGAN

Then it's true . . . ! He thought I knew. (*Laughs*) Then he said it was for the best—that I ought to be told. . . . (*The singing stops in the barn*) It is funny. She and I, we do not know each other at all. It was a long time ago, and I never thought again about it—and neither did she. I know she didn't . . . And here we are . . . It is funny, too, because if you and I had not made that bad quarrel, it would never have happened . . . It ought to make me feel older—but I feel more—young than I have ever done before . . . Oh, God, why should this happen. . . .

173

MISS MOFFAT

Steady . . .

MR. JONES

There is no need for you to upset yourself, my boy. Miss Moffat is going to take care of—of—

MORGAN

What?

MISS MOFFAT

I am going to adopt it.

MORGAN

(*His old truculent self emerging*)

What in hell do you take me for?

MR. JONES

Morgan, swearing! Be haru ti . . .

MORGAN

(*In a rage*)

I will swear some more too, if people talk to me like that! (*To* MISS MOFFAT) What do you take me for?

MR. JONES

Then what would you like to do, my boy . . . ?

MORGAN

What would I like to do? (*Getting more and more Welsh*) It is not a question of what I would like to do, or what I might be allowed, but what I am *going* to do—what any fellow with any guts in him must do! I am going to marry her!

MISS MOFFAT
(*With a cry*)
I knew this would happen, I knew . . .

MORGAN
What else is there, when I have made a fool of myself and of her, and of the poor—the poor— I am not going to talk about any of it to anybody. All I will say is that Bessie Watty and I are going to get married as soon as we can, and that is final! (*He flings himself into the armchair.*)

MISS MOFFAT
(*Hopelessly*)
I see.

(*A knock at the front door.* SARAH *hurries in agog with excitement. She runs to* MRS. WATTY.)

SARAH
Bessie's telegram from her friend, they send it from Penlan . . . I never seed one before!

MRS. WATTY
Poor chap, 'e'll be disappointed again. . . . (*Opens the telegram, and hands it to* MISS MOFFAT) What does it say, ma'am? . . . Read it, ma'am, take your mind off things . . .

(MISS MOFFAT *glances halfheartedly at the telegram. A pause. She looks up at* MORGAN.)

MISS MOFFAT

You have won the scholarship. (*Reading*) "First, Evans, Second, Fayver-Iles, Third, Starling. Congratulations." (SARAH *claps her hands and runs out by the front door, closes it.* MORGAN *laughs bitterly and turns away. Folding the telegram carefully, she tucks it into her belt, still quiet, burning with a slow-mounting and deliberate fervor*) Lock the school door, Watty, will you?

MRS. WATTY

(*To* MR. JONES, *tremulously*)

Go in there, sir, I'll make you a cup of tea. . . . (MR. JONES *goes into the kitchen.* MRS. WATTY *locks the study door and follows him.*)

MISS MOFFAT

Look at me, Morgan. (MORGAN *faces her in the armchair, defiantly*) For the first time, we are together. Our hearts are face to face, naked and unashamed, because there's no time to lose, my boy; the clock is ticking and there's no time to lose. If ever anybody has been at the crossroads, you are now. . . .

MORGAN

It is no good. I am going to marry her.

MISS MOFFAT

And I am going to speak to you very simply. I want you to change suddenly from a boy to a man. I understand that this is a great shock to you, but I want you to throw off this passionate obstinacy to do the right thing. . . . Did you promise her marriage?

MORGAN

No, never . . .

MISS MOFFAT

Did you even tell her that you were in love with her?

MORGAN

(*Repelled*)

No, never . . .

MISS MOFFAT

Then your situation now is the purest accident; it is to be regretted, but it has happened before and it will happen again. So cheer up, you are not the central figure of such a tragedy as you think . . .

MORGAN

That does not alter the fact that I have a duty to—to them both. . . .

MISS MOFFAT

She has her own plans, and she doesn't want the child; and I am willing to look after it if you behave as I want you to behave. If you marry her, you know what will happen, don't you? You will go back to the mine. In a year she will have left you—both. You will be drinking again, and this time you will not stop. And you will enjoy being this besotted and uncouth village genius who once showed such promise; but it will not be worth it, you know.

MORGAN

There is a child, living and breathing on this earth, and living and breathing because of me. . . .

MISS MOFFAT

I don't care if there are fifty children on this earth because of you! . . . You mentioned the word "duty," did you? Yes,

you have a duty, but it is not to this loose little lady, or to
her offspring either.

MORGAN

You mean a duty to you?

MISS MOFFAT

No. A year ago I should have said a duty to me, yes; but
that night you showed your teeth—you gave me a lot to think
about, you know. You caught me unawares, and I gave you
the worst possible answer back. I turned sorry for myself and
taunted you with ingratitude. I was a dolt not to realize that
a debt of gratitude is the most humiliating debt of all, and
that a little show of affection would have wiped it out. I offer
that affection to you, today.

MORGAN

Why are you saying this to me now?

MISS MOFFAT

Because, as the moments are passing, and I am going to get
my way, I know that I am never going to see you again.

(*A pause.*)

MORGAN

Never again? But why?

MISS MOFFAT

If you are not to marry her, it would be madness for you to
come into contact with the child; so if I am adopting the

178

child, you can never come to see me; it is common sense. You
have been given the push over the wall that you asked for.

MORGAN

But you—will be staying here . . . How can I never come
back—after everything you have done for me?

MISS MOFFAT

D'you remember, the last six months, I've gone for a long
walk over Moel Hiraeth, every morning at eight, like clock-
work, for my health?

MORGAN

Yes?

MISS MOFFAT

There's one bit of the road, round a boulder—and there's an
oak tree, and under it the valley suddenly drops sheer. Every
morning regularly, as I was turning that corner, by some trick
of the mind, I found myself thinking of you working for this
scholarship, and winning it. And I experienced something
which must after all be comparatively rare: A feeling—of complete happiness. I shall experience it again. No, Morgan Evans,
you have no duty to me. Your only duty—is to the world.

MORGAN

To the world?

MISS MOFFAT

Now you are going, there is no harm in telling you something. I don't think you realize quite what your future can
become if you give it the chance. I have always been very
definite about the things I wanted, and I have always had

everything worked out to a T. P'r'aps that's the trouble with me, I dunno . . . I've got *you* worked out, and it's up to you whether it will come right or not. . . .

MORGAN
(*Eagerly*)

Go on.

MISS MOFFAT

I rather made out to the Squire that I wanted you to be a writer—the truth might have sounded ridiculous; but stranger things have happened. You have a great deal now and Oxford will give you the rest.

MORGAN

For what?

MISS MOFFAT

Enough to become a great man of our country. "If a light come in the mine" you said, remember?

MORGAN

Yes.

MISS MOFFAT

Make that light come in the mine and some day free these children. And you could be more, much, much more; you could be a man for a future nation to be proud of . . . Perhaps I'm mad, I dunno. We'll see. It's up to you.

MORGAN
(*Rises before speaking*)

Yes.

(MR. JONES *appears timidly from the kitchen.*)

180

THE CORN IS GREEN

MR. JONES

Is it all right to ring the bell to say holiday tomorrow?

MISS MOFFAT

Yes. (MR. JONES's *face lights up; he hurries to the study door, unlocks it, and disappears*) I think that's all.

MORGAN

But—I—I do not know what to say.

MISS MOFFAT

Then don't say it.

MORGAN

I have been—so much time in this room.

MISS MOFFAT

And the lessons are over.

MORGAN

(*Impulsively*)

I shall—always remember.

MISS MOFFAT

Will you? Well, I'm glad you think you will. (*She presses the bag and cap into his unwilling hands.* IDWAL *runs in from the study, very excited.* ROBBART *appears behind him.*)

IDWAL

Please, Miss Moffat, the band is out, and they say Morgan